candytots

unique crochet for babies & toddlers

candi jensen

candy tots

unique crochet for babies & toddlers

candi jensen

Sixth&Spring Books
New York

Sixth&Spring Books
233 Spring St.
New York, NY 10013

Editor-in-Chief
Trisha Malcolm

Art Director
Chi Ling Moy

Photography
Dan Howell

Stylist
Mary Helt

Manager, Book Division
Theresa McKeon

Copy Editor
Michelle Lo
Jean Guirguis

Technical Editors
Carla Scott
Pat Harste

Production Manager
David Joinnides

President and Publisher, Sixth&Spring Books
Art Joinnides

Chairmen
Jay H. Stein
John E. Lehmann

Library of Congress Cataloging-in-Publication Data
Jensen, Candi
    Candy tots : unique crochet for babies and toddlers / by Candi Jensen.
                        p.cm.
            ISBN 1-931543-28-3 (pbk.)
    1. Crocheting--Patterns. 2. Infants' clothing. 3. Children's clothing. I. Title.

    TT825 .J46 2003
    746.43'40432--dc21

                                                            2002030406

            Manufactured in China

introduction

"Candy Tots" is a collection of designs inspired by two generations of crocheters—my mother and my children—and my dreams for a grandchild.

When I was a child, my mom was always busy sewing clothes for me and my sisters, and she dressed us alike as if were triplets (which was fine for me, being the youngest, but my older sisters hated dressing like a 3-year-old!). Mom had a wonderful eye for color and style and could whip up something just by looking at a picture, which she did many times, late at night, while we were sleeping. What a treat it was to wake up the next morning to her latest creations! This extraordinary experience showed me the joys of how special it was to make something creative and unique.

After I had my own children, I was inspired to create wonderful garments for them, but I did not share my mother's gift for sewing. Instead, I used my hands to knit and crochet. It was in the early '70s, when anything was possible and color, texture and especially crochet were in fashion. I made colorful one-of-a-kind sweaters for my children and they always stood out on the playground next to all the "store-bought" garments. I loved crocheting for them, but alas, they had to grow up. and I had to find other ways to keep my hands busy.

Recently, I have been inspired by the many wonderful children in my neighborhood and by the hopes of a grandchild (just a gentle suggestion). I live in a neighborhood filled with babies and

rajeana, melody and candi

toddlers, ten of them living very close by. Over the last few years, as I've watched them be born and grow, I imagined crocheting wonderful little sweaters, dresses, coats and jackets for them. That is how this book came about. They inspired me to begin creating for little ones again.

I hope all of you enjoy this book as much as I have enjoyed working on it. And another bonus: my daughter has just announced that she is having a baby! What a great gift that will be. ☆

vest friend
10/62

striped sensation
12/64

preppy preschooler
14/68

green party
16/70

simply mauve-olous
18/74

spice girl
30/86

square dance
32/88

versatile vest
34/90

pretty in pink
36/94

pompom panache
38/98

pattern play
50/116

hippie chic
52/118

wrap it up
54/122

snug as a bug
56/126

holiday magic
58/128

c o n t e n t s

Show your stripes and some fashion flair for any pint-sized outing. Deceptively easy to make, this sporty V-neck vest features simple shaping and contrast-colored edging. Stitched in a simple variation of single crochet, it works up in a jiffy with a big hook.

Crayon-colored stripes lend winsome appeal to this outstanding pullover and pompom hat ensemble. The single crochet pattern offers textural interest—this is the perfect project for using leftover yarns.

*C*heerful stripes and minimal shaping make this no-fuss project a breeze to crochet! Worked in an ultra-plush, fleece-like yarn, this trans-seasonal favorite will keep your wee one stylishly warm all-year long.

n party

That's a wrap! This snazzy single-crochet scarf and hat ensemble works up in a flash. The hat is accented with a sprightly pompom and a fold-over edge. Fringe can be added to the scarf for a more spirited look.

It's hip to be square. Lovingly rendered in vibrant colors and easy stitches, this cozy crib blanket makes an ideal companion for naptime. Worked in basic blocks, it's a practical, portable project for any crocheter on the go.

s i m p l y

u v e - o l o u s

From Sunday school to pre-school, dress your best in this adorable little design. Clever detailing such as the striped bodice, full body skirt and a cheerful daisy accent transform this dress into a stylish work of art.

f u r r e a l

No need to sacrifice style for comfort—
the sumptuous faux-fur yarn does all
the work in this plush sensation. Simply
stitch it up in single crochet and embellish
the cardigan with whimsical buttons.

A new twist on an old theme. Color and texture bow to this lofty vest in saturated hues of teal and purple. Toss this wool vest into the wash to create the felted look and feel that's oh-so cool.   ·

f r i n g e d   b e

Mix it up a little—sensational half double crochet stripes, vibrant granny squares and whimsical fringe add up to fun in this retro V-neck pullover. Dressed to impress, it offers non-stop versatility for a hip little miss.

flower power

A confection sweet poncho makes a sensible summertime cover-up when stitched with two strands of mohair/silk yarn held together. The decorative floral embellishments are knit separately, then sewn in place.

When temperatures drop, carefree accessories zap the chills away! Embellished with fringe and pompoms, this captivating set of stylish winter warmers will be a favorite all season long.

spice girl

In a kaleidoscope of jewel-tone colors, this delightful hooded coat is a dream to wear for fashion-minded tots! Vibrant granny squares are crocheted together; the coat is then completed with a simple edging.

re   d a n c e

When naptime calls, a star-spangled
baby blanket is sure to cradle
your wee one to sweet slumber. Vibrant
candy-colored stars and squares are set
against a stark black background for
dramatic contrast.

The classic argyle vest is thoroughly updated in saturated hues. A variety of colored diamonds decorate the front body and wraparound stripes provide contrast. The boxy silhouette offers all-day comfort.

tty in pink

Put a new spin on tradition. A sugary confection to crochet, this sweet V-neck pullover, a fanciful argyle pattern, features stripes along the back, chain stitch crosses and decorative bobbles on the sleeves.

p o m p o m   p a r

Two easy-stitch rectangles make up this chic argyle hat. Add a half-double crochet stripe scarf with multi-colored pompoms and he's off for a day of fun in the snow!

ache

c r o s s   m y   h e

It's off to the Emerald City! Show off her fashion sense in a snappy cotton argyle dress with colorful chain stitch patterning. A tiny ribbon threaded around the waist adds a pretty accent.

r t

n d   c h a r m

Paired with a T-shirt and jeans, this
take-everywhere cardigan is an urban
essential. Color-blocked sleeves and front
body are complemented by a richly
striped back, while a bold argyle-motif
adds dynamic interest.

Worked in easy half double crochet, this fetching little blanket is a cinch to make. A berry-colored argyle pattern stands out against the pink background, and striking purple cross-stitching makes a bold statement.

berry pr

When ease and comfort are the order for the day, your small fry can relax in this delightful pullover. Subtly shaded ribbon yarn provides ample texture and dramatic color interest to this basic pullover; a simple shell stitch-edged collar and striking silk violets add a touch of elegance.

raspb

erry rhapsody

A chic fur-trimmed coat offers no-fuss style and flare to any little girl's wardrobe. Featuring modest A-line shaping, an allover half-double crochet pattern and sumptuous fur collar and cuffs, it's truly a modern classic.

p a t t e r n   p l a y

When boys will be boys, your small tyke will earn top grades for style in this jazzy vest. Combining easy stitches with nubby textures in a palette of ocean hues, it boasts plenty of rough-and-tumble spirit.

h i p

ie chic

Yeah, Baby! Go retro with this tie-front, fur-collared vest that looks great whether paired with a tiny A-line skirt or flared bell-bottom jeans. Featuring a simple repeat of stripes and textured stitches, this vintage-inspired number is as groovy to wear as it is to crochet.

w r a p   i t   u p

Bundle up your tot against the cold of winter in a colorful pompom-trimmed hat and fringed scarf, delightfully fashioned in a bobble and textured crochet. Earflaps add extra warmth, and the tie ensures the hat stays in place. This cozy, fun-loving set works up in a flash.

s n u g   a s   a   b u g

When playtime turns into naptime,
a fringed baby blanket is in order.
Playful stripes, terrific texture and a
sophisticated palette are artfully combined
to create a noteworthy blankie that
translates into impeccable style.

Girls just want to have fun and that's what this design is all about—she'll feel like a princess in this jewel-toned treasure. The shell-stitched bodice is attached to a full-body skirt and then enhanced with a dazzling paillette trim along the empire waist.

i n s t r u c t i o n s

v e s t   f r i e n d

SIZES

Instructions are written for size 3-6 months. Changes for sizes 9-12 months, 18-24 months and 3 years are in parentheses.

FINISHED MEASUREMENTS

• Chest 22 (24, 26, 28)"/56 (61, 66, 71)cm
• Length 11 (12, 13, 14)"/28 (30.5, 33, 35.5)cm

MATERIALS

• 3 (4, 4, 5) 1¾oz/50g hanks (each approx 70yd/64m) of Classic Elite Yarns Follies (rayon/alpaca/wool ⑤) in #3402 green (MC)
• 1 hank in #3456 lavender (CC)
Size H/8 (5mm) crochet hook or size to obtain gauge

GAUGE

14 sts and 14 rows to 4"/10cm over pat st using size H/8 (5mm) hook.
Take time to check gauge.

PATTERN STITCH

(over an even number of sts)
Row 1 *Sc into front lp of next st, sc into back lp of next st; rep from * across. Ch 1, turn. Rep row 1 for pat st.

BACK

With MC, ch 39 (43, 47, 51). **Foundation row** Sc in 2nd ch from hook and in each ch across—38 (42, 46, 50) sts. Ch 1, turn. Cont in pat st and work even until piece measures 7 (7½, 8, 8½)"/17.5 (19, 20.5, 21.5)cm from beg. Do not ch, turn.
Armhole shaping
Sl st across first 4 (4, 5, 5) sts, ch 1, work in pat st across to within last 4 (4, 5, 5) sts, ch 1, turn—30 (34, 36, 40) sts. Work even until piece measures 11 (12, 13, 14)"/28 (30.5, 33, 35.5)cm from beg. Fasten off.

FRONT

Work as for back until piece measures 7½ (8, 8½, 9)"/19 (20.5, 21.5, 23)cm from beg. Ch 1, turn.
Left neck shaping
Next row Work across first 14 (16, 17, 19) sts. Ch 1, turn. Keeping to pat st, dec 1 st from neck edge every row twice, every other row 3 (4, 4, 5) times—9 (10, 11, 12) sts. Work even until same length as back. Fasten off.
Right neck shaping
Next row Sk 2 center sts, join yarn with a sc in next st, work to end. Cont to work as for left neck, reversing shaping.

FINISHING

Sew shoulder and side seams.

Neck edging

From RS, join CC with a sl st in left shoulder seam, ch 1. Making sure that work lies flat, sc around neck edge, dec 1 st over center 2 sts. Join rnd with a sl st in ch-1. Fasten off.

Armhole Edging

From RS, join CC with a sl st in underarm seam, ch 1. Making sure that work lies flat, sc around armhole edge. Join rnd with a sl st in ch-1. Fasten off.

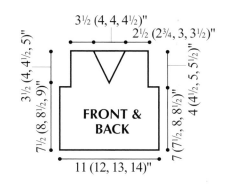

3½ (4, 4, 4½)"

2½ (2¾, 3, 3½)"

3½ (4, 4½, 5)"

4 (4½, 5, 5½)"

FRONT & BACK

7½ (8, 8½, 9)"

7 (7½, 8, 8½)"

11 (12, 13, 14)"

PULLOVER

SIZES

Instructions are written for size 3-6 months. Changes for sizes 9-12 months, 18-24 months and 3 years are in parentheses.

FINISHED MEASUREMENTS

• Chest 22 (24, 28, 30)"/56 (61, 71, 76)cm
• Length 11 (12, 14, 15)"/28 (30.5, 35.5, 38)cm
• Upper arm 9 (10, 11, 12)"/23 (25.5, 28, 30.5)cm

MATERIALS

• 1 1¾oz/50g ball (each approx 131yd/120m) of Knit One, Crochet Two Creme Brulee (machine washable wool ③) in #620 powder blue (A), #527 kiwi (B), #513 key lime (C), #101 ivory (D), #235 deep plum (E), #789 violet (F), #226 wine (G), #285 soft velvet rose (H), #359 pimento (I) and #699 soft sky blue (J)
• Size G/6 (4mm) crochet hook or size to obtain gauge
• 1 set of markers

GAUGE

18 sts and 18 rows to 4"/10cm over pat st using size G/6 (4mm) hook.
Take time to check gauge.

NOTES

1 See page 131 for making color changes.
2 You will have enough yarn left over to make a matching hat.

PATTERN STITCH

(over an even number of sts)
Row 1 *Sc into front lp of next st, sc into back lp of next st; rep from * across.
Ch 1, turn.
Rep row 1 for pat st.

STRIPE PATTERN 1

Working in pat st, work 4 rows each A, B, C, D, E, F, G, H, I, D and J.
Rep these 44 rows for stripe pat 1.

STRIPE PATTERN 2

Working in pat st, work 4 rows each I, H, G, F, E, D, C, B, A and J.
Rep these 40 rows for stripe pat 2.

BACK

With A, ch 51 (55, 65, 69). **Foundation row** Sc in 2nd ch from hook and in each ch across—50 (54, 64, 68) sts. Ch 1, turn. Work even in pat st and stripe pat 1 until piece measures 10½ (11½, 13½, 14½)"/26.5 (29, 34, 37)cm from beg.

Left shoulder

Next row Work across first 16 (18, 22, 23) sts. Ch 1, turn. Work even for 1 row. Fasten off.

Right shoulder

Next row Sk 18 (18, 20, 22) center sts, join yarn with a sc in next st, work to end. Work even for 1 more row. Fasten off.

FRONT

Work as for back until piece measures 9 (10, 11½, 12)"/23 (25.5, 29, 30.5)cm from beg. Ch 1, turn.

Left neck shaping

Next row Work across first 21 (23, 27, 29) sts. Ch 1, turn. Dec 1 st from neck edge every row 5 (5, 5, 6) times—16 (18, 22, 23) sts. Work even until same length as back. Fasten off.

Right neck shaping

Next row Sk 8 (8, 10, 10) center sts, join yarn with a sc in next st, work to end. Cont to work as for left neck, reversing shaping.

SLEEVES

With I, ch 25 (29, 29, 33). **Foundation row** Sc in 2nd ch from hook and in each ch across—24 (28, 28, 32) sts. Ch 1, turn. Work in pat st and stripe pat 2, AT SAME TIME, inc 1 st each side every other row 3 (3, 4, 4) times, every 4th row 5 (6, 7, 7) times—40 (46, 50, 54) sts. Work even until piece measures 7 (8, 9, 10)"/17.5 (20.5, 23, 25.5)cm from beg. Fasten off.

FINISHING

Sew shoulder seams.

Neck edging

From RS, join I with a sl st in left shoulder seam. Ch 1, making sure that work lies flat, sc around neck edge. Join rnd with a sl st in ch-1. Fasten off. Place markers 4½ (5, 5½, 6)"/11.5 (12.5, 14, 15)cm down from shoulder seams on front and back. Sew sleeves to armholes between markers. Sew side and sleeve seams.

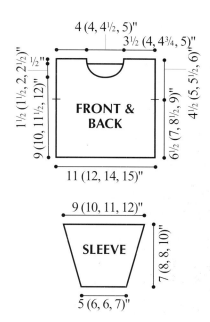

HAT

SIZES

Instructions are written for size 6-12 months. Changes for sizes 18 months-3 years are in parentheses.

FINISHED MEASUREMENTS

• Circumference 16 (19½)"/40.5 (49.5)cm

MATERIALS

• 1 1¾oz/50g ball (each approx 131yd/120m) of Knit One, Crochet Two Creme Brulee (machine washable wool ③) in #513 key lime (A), #527 kiwi (B), #620 powder blue (C), #699 soft sky blue (D), #101 ivory (E), #235 deep plum (F), #789 violet (G), #226 wine (H), #285 soft velvet rose (I) and #359 pimento (J)
• Size G/6 (4mm) crochet hook or size to obtain gauge
• Small safety pin
• 1 set of markers

GAUGE

18 sts and 18 rnds to 4"/10cm over pat st using size G/6 (4mm) hook.
Take time to check gauge.

NOTE

See page 131 for making color changes.

PATTERN STITCH

(over an even number of sts)
Rnd 1 Ch 1, *sc into front lp of next st, sc into back lp of next st; rep from * around. Join rnd with a sl st in ch-1.
Rep rnd 1 for pat st.

STRIPE PATTERN

Working in pat st, work 4 rnds each B, C, D, E, F, G, H, I, J and A.
Rep these 40 rnds for stripe pat.

HAT

With A, ch 72 (88). **Foundation rnd** Join ch with a sc forming a ring, taking care not to twist ch, then sc in each ch to end—72 (88) sts. Mark last st made with safety pin to indicate end of rnd. Work even in pat st for 3 more rnds. Cont in stripe pat and work even until piece measures 6 (8)"/15 (20)cm from beg.
Crown shaping
Take care to maintain pat st as you work dec rnds. **Dec rnd 1** *Sc in next 6 sts, dec 1 st over next 2 sts; rep from * around—63

(77) sts. Work 1 rnd even. **Dec rnd 2** *Sc in next 5 sts, dec 1 st over next 2 sts; rep from * around—54 (66) sts. Work 1 rnd even. **Dec rnd 3** *Sc in next 4 sts, dec 1 st over next 2 sts; rep from * around—45 (55) sts. Work 1 rnd even. **Dec rnd 4** *Sc in next 3 sts, dec 1 st over next 2 sts; rep from * around—36 (44) sts. Work 1 rnd even. **Dec rnd 5** *Sc in next 2 sts, dec 1 st over next 2 sts; rep from * around—27 (33) sts. Work 1 rnd even. **Dec rnd 6** *Sc in next st, dec 1 st over next 2 sts; rep from * around—18 (22) sts. Work 1 rnd even. **Dec rnd 7** *Dec 1 st over next 2 sts; rep from * around—9 (11) sts. Work 1 rnd even.

For size 18 months-3 years only

Dec rnd 8 * Sc in next st, dec 1 st over next 2 sts; rep from * around, sc in last 2 sts—8 sts. Work 1 rnd even.

For both sizes

Fasten off leaving a long tail. Thread tail into tapestry needle and weave through sts. Pull tight to gather, fasten off securely.

FINISHING

Pompom

With J, make a 2½"/6cm in diameter pompom (see pompom instructions). Sew pompom to top of hat. Fold up brim.

SIZES

Instructions are written for size 3-6 months. Changes for sizes 9-12 months, 18-24 months and 3 years are in parentheses.

FINISHED MEASUREMENTS

• Chest 22 (24, 26, 28)"/56 (61, 66, 71)cm
• Length 11 (12, 14, 15)"/28 (30.5, 35.5, 38)cm.
• Upper arm 9 (10, 11, 12)"/23 (25.5, 28, 30.5)cm

MATERIALS

• 4 (5, 5, 6) 1¾oz/50g balls (each approx 114yd/104m ⑥) of Wendy/Berroco, Inc. Velvet Touch (nylon) in #2051 amethyst (MC)
• 1 ball in #1204 lime velvet (CC)
• Size H/8 (5mm) crochet hook or size to obtain gauge
• 1 set of markers

GAUGE

12 sts and 10 rows to 4"/10cm over hdc using size H/8 (5mm) hook.
Take time to check gauge.

NOTE

See page 131 for making color changes.

BACK

With MC, ch 36 (38, 42, 44). **Foundation row** Hdc in 3rd ch from hook and in each ch across—34 (36, 40, 42) sts. Join CC, ch 2, turn. **Row 2** Hdc in each st across. Ch 2, turn. Working in hdc, work in stripe pat as foll: 1 row CC, 2 rows MC, 2 rows CC, 1 row MC and 1 row CC. Join MC, ch 2, turn. Work even until piece measures 11 (12, 14, 15)"/28 (30.5, 35.5, 38)cm from beg. Fasten off.

FRONT

Work as for back until piece measures 7 (7½, 9, 9½)"/17.5 (19, 23, 24)cm from beg. Ch 2, turn.

Left neck shaping
Next row Work across first 16 (17, 19, 20) sts. Ch 2, turn. Dec 1 st from neck edge every other row 5 (6, 6, 7) times—11 (11, 13, 13) sts. Work even until same length as back. Fasten off.
Right neck shaping
Next row Sk 2 center sts, join yarn with a

hdc in next st, work to end. Cont to work as for left neck, reversing shaping.

SLEEVES

With MC, ch 20 (22, 24, 24). **Foundation row** Hdc in 3rd ch from hook and in each ch across—18 (20, 22, 22) sts. Join CC, ch 2, turn. Working in hdc, work in stripe pat as foll: 2 rows CC, 1 row MC, 1 row CC, 2 rows MC and 1 row CC; then work with MC only, AT SAME TIME, inc 1 st each side every other row 3 times, every 4th row 2 (2, 3, 4) times—28 (30, 34, 36) sts. Work even until piece measures 7½ (8, 9, 10)"/19 (20, 23, 25.5)cm from beg. Fasten off.

FINISHING

Sew shoulder seams.

Neck edging

From RS, join CC with a sl st in left shoulder seam. **Rnd 1** Ch 1, making sure that work lies flat, sc around neck edge, dec 1 st over 2 center sts. Join rnd with a sl st in ch-1 changing to MC. **Rnd 2** Sc in each st around, dec 1 st over 2 center sts. Join rnd with a sl st in ch-1. Fasten off. Place markers 4½ (5, 5½, 6)"/11.5 (12.5, 14, 15)cm down from shoulder seams on front and back. Sew sleeves to armholes between markers. Sew side and sleeve seams.

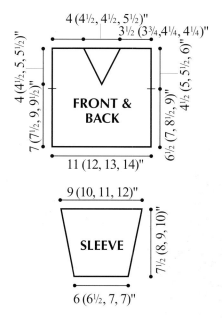

FRONT & BACK

4 (4½, 4½, 5½)"

3½ (3¾, 4¼, 4¼)"

4 (4½, 5, 5½)"

7 (7½, 9, 9½)"

6½ (7, 8½, 9)"

4½ (5, 5½, 6)"

11 (12, 13, 14)"

SLEEVE

9 (10, 11, 12)"

7½ (8, 9, 10)"

6 (6½, 7, 7)"

g r e e n p a r t y

SIZES

Instructions are written for size 6-9 months. Changes for sizes 12-24 months and 18 months-3 years are in parentheses.

FINISHED MEASUREMENTS

Hat
• Circumference 16 (18, 20)"/40.5 (45.5, 51)cm

Scarf
• 4" x 34"/10 x 86cm

MATERIALS

• 3 .85oz /25g balls (each approx 146yd/134m ⑤) of Knit One, Crochet Two Richesse et Soie (cashmere/silk) in #9512 seafoam
• Size H/8 (5mm) crochet hook or size to obtain gauge
• Small safety pin

GAUGE

14 sts and 12 rnds to 4"/10cm over pat st 1 using size H/8 (5mm) hook with 2 strands of yarn held tog.
Take time to check gauge.

NOTE

Use 2 strands of yarn held held tog throughout.

PATTERN STITCH 1

(over an even number of sts)
Rnd 1 Ch 2, *hdc into front lp of next st, hdc into back lp of next st; rep from * around. Join rnd with a sl st in 2nd ch of ch-2.
Rep rnd 1 for pat st 1.

PATTERN STITCH 2

(over any number of sts)
Rnd 1 Ch 2, hdc in each st around. Join rnd with a sl st in 2nd ch of ch-2.
Rep rnd 1 for pat st 2.

PATTERN STITCH 3

(over an even number of sts)
Row 1 *Hdc into front lp of next st, hdc into back lp of next st; rep from * to end. Ch 2, turn.
Rep row 1 for pat st 3.

HAT

With 2 strands of yarn held tog, ch 56 (64, 72). **Foundation rnd** Join ch with a hdc forming a ring, taking care not to twist ch, then hdc in each ch to end—56 (64, 72) sts. Mark last st made with safety pin to indicate end of rnd. Work even in pat st 1 until piece measures 3 (4, 5)"/7.5 (10, 12.5)cm from beg. Change to pat st 2.

Crown shaping

Dec rnd 1 *Hdc in next 6 sts, dec 1 st over next 2 sts; rep from * around—49 (56, 63) sts. Work 1 rnd even. **Dec rnd 2** *Hdc in next 5 sts, dec 1 st over next 2 sts; rep from * around—42 (48, 54) sts. Work 1 rnd even. **Dec rnd 3** *Hdc in next 4 sts, dec 1 st over next 2 sts; rep from * around—35 (40, 45) sts. Work 1 rnd even. **Dec rnd 4** *Hdc in next 3 sts, dec 1 st over next 2 sts; rep from * around—28 (32, 36) sts. Work 1 rnd even. **Dec rnd 5** *Hdc in next 2 sts, dec 1 st over next 2 sts; rep from * around—21 (24, 27) sts. Work 1 rnd even. **Dec rnd 6** *Hdc in next st, dec 1 st over next 2 sts; rep from * around—14 (16, 18) sts. Work 1 rnd even. **Dec rnd 7** *Dec 1 st over next 2 sts; rep from * around—7 (8, 9) sts. Fasten off leaving a long tail. Thread tail into tapestry needle and weave through sts. Pull tight to gather; fasten off securely.

FINISHING

Pompom

Make a 2½"/6cm in diameter pompom (see pompom instructions). Sew pompom to top of hat. Fold up brim.

SCARF

With 2 strands of yarn held tog, ch 14. **Foundation row** Hdc in 3rd ch from hook and in each ch across—12 sts. Ch 2, turn. Cont in pat st 3 and work even until piece measures 34"/86cm from beg. Fasten off.

FINISHED MEASUREMENTS
• 32" x 32"/81 x 81cm

MATERIALS
• 3 5oz/140g skeins (each approx 253yd/231m) of Red Heart/Coats & Clark TLC (acrylic ⑤) in #5823 medium blue (MC)
• 2 skeins #5507 bright jade (A)
• 1 skein #5657 kiwi (B)
• Size I/9 (5.5mm) crochet hook or size to obtain gauges
• 3" x 5"/7.5 x 12.5cm piece of cardboard (for tassels)

GAUGES
• 14 sts and 13 rows to 4"/10cm over pat st using size I/9 (5.5mm) hook.
• One square to 8"/20cm using size I/9 (5.5mm) hook.
Take time to check gauges.

NOTE
See page 131 for making color changes.

PATTERN STITCH
(over an even number of sts)
Row 1 *Sc into front lp of next st, sc into back lp of next st; rep from * across.
Ch 1, turn.
Rep row 1 for pat st.

SQUARE 1
(make 6)
With A, ch 19. **Foundation row (RS)** Sc in 2nd ch from hook and in each ch across—18 sts. Ch 1, turn. Cont in pat st and work even for 15 rows, end with a WS row. Fasten off. Turn work.
Border
From RS, join MC with a sl in first st of last row worked, ch 1 (counts as 1 sc). **Rnd 1** Work 16 sc evenly spaced across each side, working 3 sc in each corner—76 sts. Join rnd with a sl st in ch-1. **Rnds 2-4** Ch 1, keeping to pat st, sc in each st around, working 3 sc in back lp of each corner st around. Join rnd with a sl st in ch-1. When rnd 4 is completed you will have 100 sts (22 sts across each side and 3 sts in each corner). Fasten off.

SQUARE 2
(make 6)
With A, ch 13. **Foundation row (RS)** Sc in 2nd ch from hook and in each ch across—12 sts. Ch 1, turn. Cont in pat st and work even for 9 rows, end with a WS row. Fasten off. Turn work.
Border
From RS, join MC with a sl in first st of last row worked, ch 1 (counts as 1 sc). **Rnd 1** Work 10 sc evenly spaced across each side, working 3 sc in each corner—52 sts. Join rnd with a sl st in ch-1. **Rnds 2-7** Ch 1, keeping to pat st, sc in each st around, working 3 sc in back lp of each corner st around. Join rnd with a sl st in ch-1. When rnd 7 is completed you will have 100 sts. Fasten off.

SQUARE 3
(make 4)
With B, ch 9. **Foundation row (RS)** Sc in

2nd ch from hook and in each ch across—8 sts. Ch 1, turn. Cont in pat st and work even for 5 rows, end with a WS row. Fasten off. Turn work.

Border

From RS, join B with a sl in first st of last row worked, ch 1 (counts as 1 sc). **Rnd 1** Work 6 sc evenly spaced across each side, working 3 sc in each corner—36 sts. Join rnd with a sl st in ch-1. **Rnds 2-3** Ch 1, keeping to pat st, sc in each st around, working 3 sc in back lp of each corner st around. Join rnd with a sl st in ch-1. When rnd 3 is completed you will have 52 sts (10 sts across each side and 3 sts in each corner). Join MC. **Rnds 4-9** Ch 1, keeping to pat st, sc in each st around, working 3 sc in back lp of each corner st around. Join rnd with a sl st in ch-1. When rnd 9 is completed you will have 100 sts. Fasten off.

FINISHING

Referring to photo, use MC to sew squares tog forming rows, then sew rows tog forming blanket.

Tassels

(make 4)

Wrap C 32 times around cardboard. Slip a 10"/25.5cm-length of C under strands and tightly knot at one end of cardboard. Remove cardcoard. Wrap and tie another length of yarn around the tassel about 1"/2.5cm down from the top. Cut loops at opposite ends. Trim ends even. Sew one tassel to each corner of blanket.

SIZES

Instructions are written for size 3-6 months. Changes for sizes 9-12 months, 18-24 months and 3 years are in parentheses.

FINISHED MEASUREMENTS

- Chest 18 (20, 22, 24)"/45.5 (51, 56, 61)cm
- Length 14 (16, 19, 22)"/35.5 (40.5, 48, 56)cm

MATERIALS

- 2 (2, 2, 3) 4.4oz/125g ball (each approx 256yd/234m) of Classic Elite Yarns Provence (cotton ⑤) in #2654 english lilac (MC)
- 1 ball each in #2632 mad magenta (A), #2672 gentle green (B) and #2674 fiddlehead (C)
- Size H/8 (5mm) crochet hook or size to obtain gauge
- Small safety pin

GAUGE

16 sts and 16 rows to 4"/10cm over pat st 1 using size H/8 (5mm) hook.
Take time to check gauge.

NOTES

1 See page 131 for making color changes.
2 Front and back are made separately, then sewn tog.
3 Skirt is made in one piece from bodice to hem.

PATTERN STITCH 1

(over an even number of sts)
Row 1 *Sc into front lp of next st, sc into back lp of next st; rep from * across. Ch 1, turn.
Rep row 1 for pat st 1.

PATTERN STITCH 2

(over an even number of sts)
Rnd 1 Ch 1, *sc into front lp of next st, sc into back lp of next st; rep from * around. Join rnd with a sl st in ch-1.
Rep rnd 1 for pat st 2.

STRIPE PATTERN

Working in pat st 1, work 2 rows each A, B, C and MC.
Rep these 8 rows for stripe pat.

BACK BODICE

With MC, ch 37 (41, 45, 49). **Foundation row** Sc in 2nd ch from hook and in each ch across—36 (40, 44, 48) sts. Ch 1, turn. Cont in pat st 1 for 1 row. Join A, ch 1, turn. Cont in stripe pat and work even until piece measures 1 (1½, 2, 2½)"/2.5 (4, 5, 6)cm from beg. Do not ch, turn.
Armhole shaping
Sl st across first 2 (2, 3, 3) sts, ch 1, work across to within last 2 (2, 3, 3) sts, ch 1, turn—32 (36, 38, 42) sts. Dec 1 st each side every row 2 (2, 2, 3) times—28 (32, 34, 36) sts. Work even until piece measures 2½ (3, 4, 4½)"/6 (7.5, 10, 11.5)cm from beg. Ch 1, turn.

Left neck shaping

Next row Work across first 11 (13, 13, 14) sts. Ch 1, turn. Dec 1 st from neck edge every row 3 (4, 4, 4) times—8 (9, 9, 10) sts. Work even until piece measures 4 (5, 6, 7)"/10 (12.5, 15, 17.5)cm from beg. Fasten off.

Right neck shaping

Next row Sk 6 (6, 8, 8) center sts, join yarn with a sc in next st, work to end. Cont to work as for left neck, reversing shaping.

FRONT BODICE

Work as for back bodice. Sew shoulder and side seams.

SKIRT

With RS facing, join MC with a sl st in left side seam. **Foundation rnd** Ch 1, working in bottom lps of foundation ch, sc in each bottom lp around—72 (80, 88, 96) sts. Mark last st made with the safety pin to indicate end of rnd. Join rnd with a sl st in ch-1, changing to C. **Inc rnd** *Work 2 sc in next st, sc in next st; rep from * around— 108 (120,132,144) sts. Join rnd with a sl st in ch-1, changing to B. Cont in pat st 2 and work even for 2 rnds, changing to A after 2nd rnd. Work 2 rnds even, changing

to MC after 2nd rnd. Cont to work even in pat st 2 until skirt measures 10 (11, 13, 15)"/25.5 (28, 33, 38)cm from beg. Fasten off.

FINISHING

Neck edging

With RS facing, join A with a sl st in left shoulder seam. **Rnd 1** Ch 1, making sure that work lies flat, sc evenly around. Join rnd with a sl st in ch-1. Fasten off.

Armhole edging

With RS facing, join A with a sl st in side seam. **Rnd 1** Ch 1, making sure that work lies flat, sc evenly around. Join rnd with a sl st in ch-1. Fasten off.

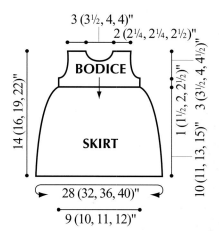

f u r   r e a l

SIZES

Instructions are written for size 3-6 months. Changes for sizes 9-12 months, 18-24 months and 3 years are in parentheses.

FINISHED MEASUREMENTS

• Chest (buttoned) 22 (24, 26, 28)"/56 (61, 66, 71)cm
• Length 11 (12, 13, 14)"/28 (30.5, 33, 35.5)cm
• Upper arm 10 (11, 11½, 12)"/25.5 (28, 29, 30.5)cm

MATERIALS

• 4 (5, 5, 6) 3½oz/100g hanks (each approx 150yd/137m) of Friends, Inc. Mustachio (acrylic ⑥) in #03 burgundy
• Size I/9 (5.5mm) crochet hook or size to obtain gauge
• Three ⅞"/22mm buttons
• 1 set of markers

GAUGE

11 sts and 10 rows to 4"/10cm over sc using size I/9 (5.5mm) hook.
Take time to check gauge.

NOTE

It is sometimes difficult seeing the sts when working with furry yarn. For best results, count sts as you work across each row to make sure you do not skip or miss a st.

BACK

Ch 31 (35, 37, 39). **Row 1** Sc in 2nd ch from hook and in each ch across—30 (34, 36, 38) sts. Ch 1, turn. **Row 2** Sc in each st across. Ch 1, turn. Rep row 2 for pat st and work even until piece measures 11 (12, 13, 14)"/28 (30.5, 33, 35.5)cm from beg. Fasten off.

LEFT FRONT

Ch 17 (19, 20, 22). **Row 1** Sc in 2nd ch from hook and in each ch across—16 (18, 19, 21) sts. Ch 1, turn. Work even in sc until piece measures 7 (7½, 8, 8½)"/17.5 (19, 20.5, 21.5)cm from beg.
Neck shaping
Next row (RS) Work across to last 2 sts, dec 1 st over last 2 sts. Cont to dec 1 st from same edge every row 4 (5, 6, 7) times more—11 (12, 12, 13) sts. Work even until piece measures same length as back. Fasten off.

RIGHT FRONT

Work as for left front reversing neck shaping.

SLEEVES

Ch 17 (19, 21, 23). **Row 1** Sc in 2nd ch from hook and in each ch across—16 (18, 20, 22) sts. Ch 1, turn. Work in sc and inc 1 st each side every other row 6 times—28 (30, 32, 34) sts. Work even until piece measures 7 (8, 9, 10)"/17.5 (20, 23, 25.5)cm from beg. Fasten off.

FINISHING

Sew shoulder seams. Place markers 5 (5½, 5¾, 6)"/12.5 (14, 14.5, 15)cm down from shoulder seams on fronts and back. Sew sleeves to armholes between markers. Sew side and sleeve seams.

Button loops

(make 3)

Ch 8. Fasten off leaving a long tail for sewing. Fold ch in half to make loop. On right front, sew first loop at beg of neck shaping and the others spaced 2"/5cm apart. Sew on buttons.

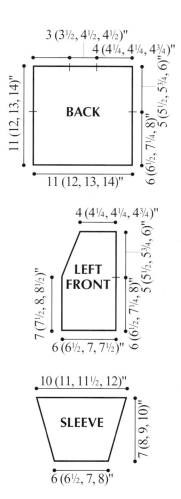

SIZES

Instructions are written for size 6-12 months. Changes for sizes 24 months-3 years are in parentheses.

FINISHED MEASUREMENTS

- Chest 25 (30)"/63.5 (76)cm
- Length 12½ (15)"/31.5 (38)cm

MATERIALS

- *1 3½oz /100g hanks (each approx 200yd/183m) of Brown Sheep Co. Lamb's Pride Worsted (wool ④) in #M59 periwinkle (A) and #M78 aztec turquoise (B)*
- *Size G/6 (4mm) crochet hook (for size 6-12 months) or size to obtain gauge*
- *Size I/9 (5.5mm) crochet hook (for size 24 months-3 years) or size to obtain gauge*
- *Baking soda and detergent (for felting)*

GAUGES

- One square to 2½"/6cm using size G/6 (4mm) hook after felting.
- One square to 3"/7.5cm using size I/9 (5.5mm) hook after felting.

Take time to check gauge.

NOTE

See page 132 for granny square basics.

FELTING

Make one extra granny square for gauge swatch to test felting. Fill washing machine to low water setting at a hot temperature (approx 100-110ºF/40-45ºC). Add ⅛ cup of baking soda and ¼ to ½ cup detergent. Add a small towel to provide abrasion and balanced agitation. Use 10-12 minute wash cycle, including cold rinse and spin. Check to see if the approx gauge has been achieved, if not, rep process with progressively shorter cycles. Cont to check every few minutes until you achieve stated gauge. Record details of water amount, temperatures and cycle lengths for felting completed vest.

SQUARE 1

(make 29)
Work as for multi-color basic granny square working rnd 1 with A and rnd 2 with B.

SQUARE 2

(make 10)
Work as for multi-color basic granny square working rnd 1 with B and rnd 2 with A.

SQUARE 3

(make 1)
Work as for solid color basic granny square working rnds 1 and 2 with A.

HALF-SQUARE

(make 4)

Work as for multi-color basic granny half-square working row 1 with A and row 2 with B.

FINISHING

Referring to placement diagram, sew squares and half-squares tog. Sew shoulder and side seams.

Neck edging

From RS, join A with a sl st in left shoulder seam. **Rnd 1** Ch 1, making sure that work lies flat, sc around neck edge. Join rnd with a sl st in ch-1. Fasten off. Rep edging around each armhole and bottom edge.

Felting

Rep process using high water setting, a large towel and proportionate amount of detergent (at least ¼ cup baking soda and 1 cup detergent). Run through one normal cycle. Check vest frequently for signs of felting and if gauge for squares has been achieve. Proceed as for gauge swatch, but note that due to difference in size and weight, vest may felt much quicker than swatch. Remove vest when you get proper texture and size. Run through spin cycle to remove excess water. Lie vest flat on towel to dry; change to a fresh towel when needed. Some blocking may be done by patting and stretching.

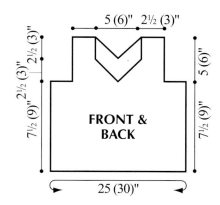

FRONT & BACK

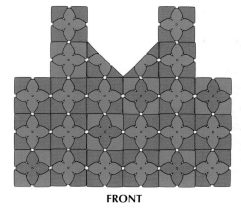

FRONT

Color Key
- Periwinkle (A)
- Aztec turquoise (B)

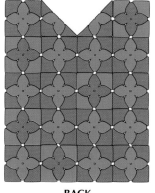

BACK

f r i n g e d   b e n e f i t

SIZES

Instructions are written for size 3-6 months. Changes for sizes 12-24 months and 3 years are in parentheses.

FINISHED MEASUREMENTS

- Chest 20 (25, 30)"/51 (63.5, 76)cm
- Length 11 (13, 15)"/28 (33, 38)cm (not including tassels)
- Upper arm 8 (10, 12)"/20 (25.5, 30.5)cm

MATERIALS

- 2 (2, 3) 1¾oz /50g balls (each approx 131yd/120m) of Knit One, Crochet Two Creme Brulee (wool ③) in #235 deep plum (A)
- 1 ball each in #789 violet (B), #620 powder blue (C), #527 kiwi (D) and #513 key lime (E)
- Size G/6 (4mm) crochet hook or size to obtain gauges
- 3¼ x 3¼"/8 x 8cm piece of cardboard (for tassels)
- 1 set of markers

GAUGES

- 16 sts and 13 rows to 4"/10cm over hdc using size G/6 (4mm) hook.
- One square to 5"/12.5cm using size G/6 (4mm) hook.

Take time to check gauges.

NOTES

1 See page 132 for granny square basics.

2 See page 131 for making color changes.

STRIPE PATTERN

Work 1 row each C, D, E, A and B. Rep these 5 rows for stripe pat.

BACK

With A, ch 42 (52, 62). **Row 1** Hdc in 3rd ch from hook and in each ch across—40 (50, 60) sts. Join B, ch 2, turn. **Row 2** Hdc in each st across. Join C, ch 2, turn. Cont in hdc and in stripe pat, and work even until piece measures 6 (8, 10)"/15 (20, 25.5)cm from beg. Fasten off.

FRONT

Work as for back until piece measures 2½ (4, 5½)"/6 (10, 14)cm from beg.

Left neck shaping

Next row Work across 19 (24, 29) sts, join next color, ch 2, turn. Dec 1 st from neck edge every row 6 (7, 9) times—13 (17, 20) sts. Work even until same length as back. Fasten off.

Right neck shaping

Next row Sk 2 center sts, join next color with a hdc in next st, work to end. Cont to work as for left neck, reversing shaping.

SLEEVES

With A, ch 26 (30, 34). **Row 1** Hdc in 3rd ch from hook and in each ch across—24 (28, 32) sts. Join B, ch 2, turn. **Row 2** Hdc in each st across. Join C, ch 2, turn. Cont in hdc and stripe pat, AT SAME TIME, inc 1 st each side every other row 4 (6, 8) times—32 (40, 48) sts. Work even until piece measures 6 (8, 9)"/15 (20, 23)cm from beg. Fasten off.

GRANNY SQUARES

Make 4 (5, 6). Work as for multi-color basic granny square working rnd 1 with E, rnd 2 with D, rnd 3 with C, rnd 4 with B and rnd 5 with A.

FINISHING

Sew shoulder seams. Place markers 4 (5, 6)"/10 (12.5, 15)cm down from shoulder seams on front and back. Sew sleeves to armholes between markers. Sew side and sleeve seams. Sew squares tog forming a ring.

For sizes 3-6 months and 3 years only
Sew squares to bottom edge of front and back, matching side seams.
For size 12-24 months only
Sew squares to bottom edge of front and back, positioning a square at center front.
Neck edging
From RS, join A with a sl st in left shoulder seam. **Rnd 1** Ch 1, making sure that work lies flat, sc around neck edge, dec 1 st over center 2 sts. Join rnd with a sl st in ch-1. Fasten off.
Tassels

Make 20 (25, 30). Wrap A 11 times around cardboard. Slip a 10"/25.5cm-length of A under strands and tightly knot at one end of cardboard. Remove cardboard. Wrap and tie another length of yarn around the tassel about ¾"/2cm down from the top. Cut loops at opposite ends. Trim ends even. Sew tassels around bottom edge, as shown.

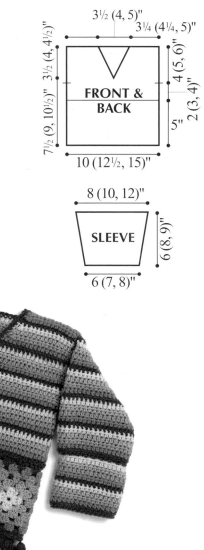

FRONT & BACK

3½ (4, 5)"
3¼ (4¼, 5)"
7½ (9, 10½)"
3½ (4, 4½)"
4 (5, 6)"
5"
2 (3, 4)"
10 (12½, 15)"

SLEEVE

8 (10, 12)"
6 (8, 9)"
6 (7, 8)"

f l o w e r   p o w e r

SIZE

Instructions are written for size 18 months-3 years.

FINISHED MEASUREMENTS

• Rectangle 10" x 20"/25.5 x 51cm

MATERIALS

• 2 .85oz /25g balls (each approx 225yd/206m) of Knit One, Crochet Two Douceur et Soie (mohair/silk ⑤) each in #8243 soft sunrise (A) and #8248 velvet rose (B)
• Size I/9 (5.5mm) crochet hook (for poncho) or size to obtain gauge
• Size G/6 (4mm) crochet hook (for flowers) or size to obtain gauge

GAUGES

• 12 sts and 8 rows to 4"/10cm over dc using size I/9 (5.5mm) hook and 2 strands of yarn held tog.

• One flower to 4¾"/12cm using size G/6 (4mm) hook and 2 strands of yarn held tog.
Take time to check gauges.

NOTE

Use 2 strands of yarn held tog throughout.

PONCHO

(make 2 pieces)
With larger hook and one strand each of A and B held tog, ch 33. **Row 1** Dc in 4th ch from hook and in each ch across—30 sts. Ch 3, turn. **Row 2** Dc in each st across. Ch 3, turn. Rep row 2 for pat st and work even until piece measures 20"/51cm from beg. Fasten off.

FLOWERS

(make 16)
With smaller hook and 2 strands of A, ch 5. Join ch with a sl st forming a ring.

Rnd 1 Ch 1, work 16 sc over ring. Join rnd with a sl st in ch-1. **Rnd 2** [Ch 4, sk next 2 sts, sl st in next st] 5 times, end ch 4, sk last 2 sts, sl st in first ch of ch-4—6 ch-4 lps. **Rnd 3** Ch 1 (counts as 1 sc), work (4 dc, 1 tr, 4 dc, sc) in first ch-4 sp, * work (sc, 4 dc, 1 tr, 4 dc, sc) in next ch-4 sp; rep from * around 5 times. Join rnd with a sl st in ch-1. **Rnd 4** [Ch 5, sl st between next 2 sc (between petals)] 5 times, end ch 5, sl st in first ch of beg ch-5—6 ch-5 lps. Fasten off. **Rnd 5** Join 2 strands of B with a sl st in any ch-5 lp, ch 1, *work (sc, 5 dc, 3 tr, 5dc, sc) in next ch-5 lp; rep from * around 6 times. Join rnd with a sl st in ch-1. Fasten off.

FINISHING

Sew bottom edge of one poncho piece to side edge of second piece, outer side edges even. Sew opposite ends in the same manner forming "V".

Neck edging

From RS, with larger hook and A and B held tog, join yarn with a sl st in center back neck edge. **Rnd 1** Ch 1, making sure that work lies flat, sc around neck edge. Join rnd with a sl st in ch-1. Fasten off. Sew flowers onto poncho, as shown.

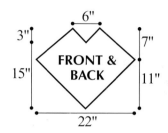

FRONT & BACK

6"
3"
7"
15"
11"
22"

SIZES

Instructions are written for size 6-12 months. Changes for sizes 18 months-3 years are in parentheses.

FINISHED MEASUREMENTS
Hat
- Circumference 17 (19)"/43 (48)cm

Scarf
- 5" x 30"/12.5 x 76cm (not including fringe)

MATERIALS
- *2 (2, 3, 3) 1¾oz /50g balls (each approx 131yd/120m) of Knit One, Crochet Two Creme Brulee (wool ③) in #235 deep plum (E)*
- *1 ball each in #513 key lime (A), #527 kiwi (B), #620 powder blue (C) and #789 violet (D)*
- *Size G/6 (4mm) crochet hook or size to obtain gauges*

GAUGES
- 16 sts and 12 rnds to 4"/10cm over hdc using size G/6 (4mm) hook.
- One square to 5"/12.5cm using size G/6 (4mm) hook.

Take time to check gauges.

NOTES
1 See page 131 for making color changes.
2 See page 132 for granny square basics.

STRIPE PATTERN
Work 1 row each C, D, E, A and B.
Rep these 5 rows for stripe pat.

HAT
Brim
With A, ch 70 (78). **Row 1** Hdc in 3rd ch from hook and in each ch across—68 (76) sts. Join B, ch 2, turn. **Row 2** Hdc in each st across. Join C, ch 2, turn. Cont in hdc and stripe pat, and work even until piece measures 4 (5)"/10 (12.5)cm from beg.

For size 6-12 months only
Next row *Hdc in next 10 sts, work 2 hdc in next st; rep from * across, end hdc in last 2 sts—74 sts. **Next row** *Hdc in next 11 sts, work 2 hdc in next st; rep from * across, end hdc in last 2 sts—80 sts. Fasten off.

For size 18 months-3 years only
Next row *Hdc in next 18 sts, work 2 hdc in next st; rep from * across—80 sts.
Fasten off.

For both sizes

Work even until piece measures 5 (6)"/12.5 (15)cm frm beg. Fasten off.

GRANNY SQUARES

(make 4)

Work as for multi-color basic granny square working rnd 1 with A, rnd 2 with B, rnd 3 with C, rnd 4 with D and rnd 5 with E.

FINISHING

Sew squares tog forming a strip. Sew brim to strip. Sew side seam. Working from the side in, sew top edges of squares tog halfway; they will all meet in the center forming 4 points.

Pompoms

(make 4)

Using all colors, make a 2¼"/6cm in diameter pompom (see pompom instructions). Sew a pompom to each point, as shown. Fold back brim.

SCARF

Make 6 granny squares as for hat.

FINISHING

Sew squares tog forming a strip.

Fringe

For each fringe, cut each color 6"/15cm long. Use hook to pull through and knot fringe. At each end of scarf, knot 6 fringe across.

spice girl

SIZES

Instructions are written for size 6-12 months. Changes for sizes 24 months-3 years are in parentheses.

FINISHED MEASUREMENTS

• Chest (buttoned) 24 (30)"/61 (76)cm
• Length 16 (20)"/40.5 (51)cm
• Upper arm 10 (12½)"/25.5 (31.5)cm

MATERIALS

• 6 (8) 1¾oz /50g balls (each approx 110yd/100m) of Noro Kureyon (wool ④) in #102 fuchsia brights
• Size G/6 (4mm) crochet hook (for size 6-12 months) or size to obtain gauge
• Size I/9 (5.5mm) crochet hook (for size 24 months-3 years) or size to obtain gauge
• Three ⅞"/22mm buttons
• 1 set of markers

GAUGES

• One square to 2"/5cm using size G/6 (4mm) hook.
• One square to 2½"/6cm using size I/9 (5.5mm) hook.
Take time to check gauge.

NOTE

See page 132 for granny square basics.

GRANNY SQUARES

(make 158)
Work as for solid color basic granny square working rnds 1 and 2.

HALF-SQUARES

(make 2)
Work as for basic granny half-square.

QUARTER-SQUARES

(make 8)
Work as for basic granny quarter-square.

FINISHING

Refer to placement diagrams. Sew squares tog to form back and hood. Sew squares and half-squares tog to form fronts. Sew squares and quarter-squares tog to form sleeves. Sew shoulder seams. Place markers 5 (6¼)"/12.5 (16)cm down from shoulder seams on fronts and back. Sew sleeves to armholes between markers. Sew side and sleeve seams. Fold hood in half and sew back seam. Sew hood to neck edge, beg and ending above half-square at each neck edge and easing in fullness along neck edge.

Edging

From RS, join yarn with a sl st in left side seam, ch 1. Making sure that work lies flat, sc around entire edge working 3 sc in each corner. Join rnd with a sl st in ch-1. Fasten off.

Button loops

(make 3)

Ch 8. Fasten off leaving a long tail for sewing. Fold ch in half to make loop. On right front, sew first loop at base of half-square at neck and the others spaced 2 (2½)"/5 (6)cm apart. Sew on buttons.

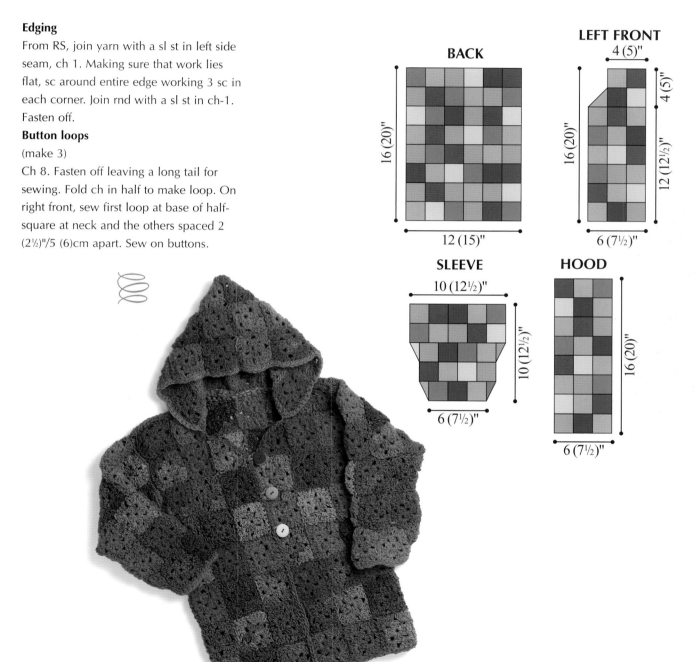

BACK

16 (20)"

12 (15)"

LEFT FRONT

4 (5)"

4 (5)"

16 (20)"

12 (12½)"

6 (7½)"

SLEEVE

10 (12½)"

10 (12½)"

6 (7½)"

HOOD

16 (20)"

6 (7½)"

s q u a r e   d a n c e

FINISHED MEASUREMENTS
28" x 28"/71 x 71cm (not including edging)

MATERIALS
• 2 5oz/140g skeins (each approx 253yd/231m) of Red Heart/Coats & Clark TLC (acrylic ⑤) in #5012 black (MC)
• 1 skein each in #5289 copper (A), #5507 bright jade (B), #5657 kiwi (C), #5263 butterscotch (D), #5768 fuchsia (E) and #5585 lavender (F)
• Size J/10 (6mm) crochet hook or size to obtain gauge

GAUGE
One square to 2¾"/7cm using size J/10 (6mm) hook.
Take time to check gauge.

NOTE
See page 132 for granny square basics.

TWO-COLOR SQUARES 1
(make 76)
Work as for multi-color basic granny square working rnd 1 with A, B, C, D, E or F, and rnd 2 with MC. Make 12 each in A, B and C, 13 each in D and E, and 14 in F.

TWO-COLOR SQUARES 2
(make 18)
Work as for multi-color basic granny square working rnd 1 with MC and rnd 2 with A, B, C, D, E or F. Make 3 in each color.

SOLID-COLOR SQUARES
(make 6)
Work rnds 1 and 2 as for solid color basic granny square. Make 1 each in A, B, C, D, E and F.

FINISHING
Referring to photo, use MC to sew squares tog forming rows, then sew rows tog forming blanket.

Edging
From RS, join MC with sl st in any ch-1 sp. **Rnd 1** Ch 1 (counts as 1 sc), sc in each st and ch-1 sp around, working 3 sc in each corner ch-2 sp. Join rnd with a sl st in ch-1. **Rnd 2** Ch 1, sc in each st around, working 3 sc in each corner sc. Join rnd with a sl st in ch-1. Fasten off.

v e r s a t i l e   v e s t

SIZES

Instructions are written for size 3-6 months. Changes for sizes 9-12 months, 18-24 months and 3 years are in parentheses.

FINISHED MEASUREMENTS

• Chest 22 (24, 26, 28)"/56 (61, 66, 71)cm
• Length 12 (13, 14, 15)"/30.5 (33, 35.5, 38)cm

MATERIALS

• 2 1¾oz/50g balls (each approx 138yd/126m) of Classic Elite Yarbs Waterspun (wool ④) in #5036 lime green (A)
• 1 ball each in #5049 blue (B), #5035 olive green (C), #5046 teal blue (D), #5027 red purple (E) and #5068 orange (F)
• Size H/8 (5mm) crochet hook or size to obtain gauge
• Nine bobbins

GAUGE

16 sts and 16 rows to 4"/10cm over pat st using size H/8 (5mm) hook.
Take time to check gauge.

NOTES

1 See page 131 for working color changes for argyle patterns.
2 Wind A onto 5 bobbins and B, C, D and E onto separate bobbins.
3 See page 131 for working color changes for rows.
4 See page 133 for embroidering chain-stitch.

PATTERN STITCH

Row 1 Sc in back lp of each st across. Ch 1, turn.
Rep row 1 for pat st.

STRIPE PATTERN

Working in pat st, work 1 row each B, C, D, E, F and A.
Rep these 6 rows for stripe pat.

BACK

With A, ch 53 (57, 65, 69). **Foundation row** Sc in 2nd ch from hook and in each ch across—52 (56, 64, 68) sts. Join B, ch 1, turn. Cont in pat st and stripe pat and work even until piece measures 7½ (8, 8½,

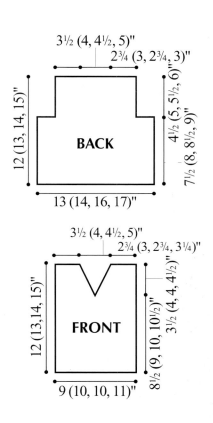

3½ (4, 4½, 5)"

2¾ (3, 2¾, 3)"

12 (13, 14, 15)"

4½ (5, 5½, 6)"

7½ (8, 8½, 9)"

BACK

13 (14, 16, 17)"

3½ (4, 4½, 5)"

2¾ (3, 2¾, 3¼)"

12 (13,14, 15)"

3½ (4, 4, 4½)"

FRONT

8½ (9, 10, 10½)"

3½ (4, 4, 4½)"

9 (10, 10, 11)"

9)"/19 (20, 21.5, 23)cm from beg. Fasten off. Turn work.

Armhole shaping

Next row Keeping to stripe pat, sk first 8 (8, 12, 12) sts, join next color with a sc in next st, work across to within last 8 (8, 12, 12) sts. Join next color, ch 1, turn—36 (40, 40, 44) sts. Work even until piece measures 12 (13, 14,15)"/30.5 (33, 35,5, 38)cm from beg. Fasten off.

FRONT

With A, ch 37 (41, 41, 45). **Foundation row** Sc in 2nd ch from hook and in each ch across—36 (40, 40, 44) sts. Ch 1, turn. Cont in pat st.

Beg chart

Row 5 (5, 3, 1) Beg with st 5 (3, 3, 1) and work to st 40 (42, 42, 44). Cont to foll chart in this way until row 42 is completed.

Left neck shaping

Row 43 (RS) Work across first 17 (19, 19, 21) sts, ch 1 turn. Dec 1 st from neck edge every row 4 times, every other row 2 (3, 4, 5) times—11 (12, 11, 12) sts. Work even

until row 56 (58, 58, 60) is completed. Fasten off.

Right neck shaping

Row 43 (RS) Keeping to chart pat, sk 2 center sts, join yarn with a sc in next st, work to end. Cont to work as for left neck, reversing shaping.

FINISHING

Embroidery

Referring to chart, use F to embroider chain-stitch diagonal lines. Sew shoulder and side seams.

Neck edging

From RS, join E with a sl st in left shoulder seam. **Rnd 1** Ch 1, making sure that work lies flat, sc around neck edge. Join rnd with a sl st in ch-1. Fasten off. Rep edging around each armhole and bottom edge.

Color Key

☐ Lime (A)

▨ Blue (B)

▨ Olive (C)

■ Teal blue (D)

■ Red purple (E)

⊡ Orange (F) chain st

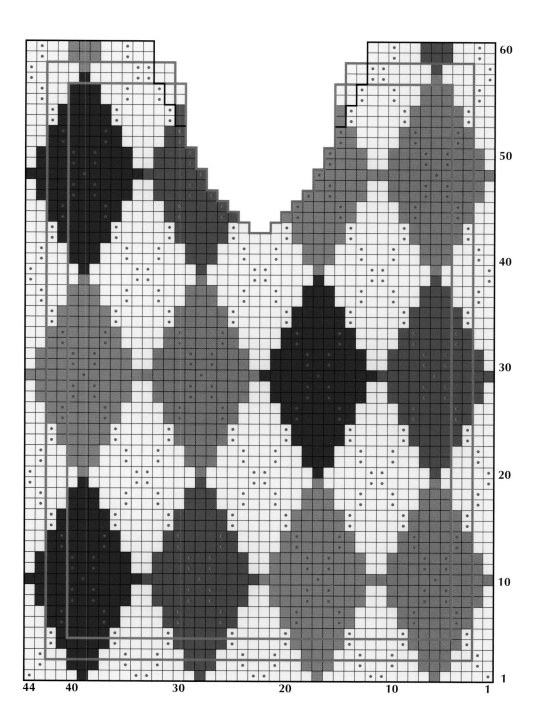

SIZES

Instructions are written for size 3-6 months. Changes for sizes 9-12 months, 18-24 months and 3 years are in parentheses.

FINISHED MEASUREMENTS

• Chest 22 (24, 26, 28)"/56 (61, 66, 71)cm
• Length 12 (13, 14, 15)"/30.5 (33, 35.5, 38)cm
• Upper arm 9 (10, 11, 12)"/23 (25.5, 28, 30.5)cm

MATERIALS

• 3 (4, 4, 5) 1¾oz/50g balls (each approx 136yd/124m) of Patons Grace (cotton ③) in #60416 blush (A)
• 2 balls in #60437 rose (B)
• 1 ball each in #60450 coral (C), #60409 ruby (D) and #60321 viola (E)
• Size G/6 (4mm) crochet hook or size to obtain gauge
• Eleven bobbins

GAUGE

20 sts and 20 rows to 4"/10cm over pat st using size G/6 (4mm) hook.
Take time to check gauge.

NOTES

1 See page 131 for working color changes for argyle patterns.
2 Wind A onto 5 bobbins, and C and D onto 3 bobbins each.
3 See page 131 for working color changes for rows.

4 See page 133 for embroidering chain-stitch.

PATTERN STITCH

Row 1 Sc in back lp of each st across. Ch 1, turn.
Rep row 1 for pat st.

STRIPE PATTERN

Working in pat st, work 1 row B and 1 row A. Rep these 2 rows for stripe pat.

BACK

With A, ch 67 (73, 83, 87). **Foundation row** Sc in 2nd ch from hook and in each ch across—66 (72, 82, 86) sts. Change to B, ch 1, turn. Cont in pat st and stripe pat and work even until piece measures 7½ (8, 8½, 9)"/19 (20, 21.5, 23)cm from beg. Fasten off. Turn work.

Armhole shaping

Next row Keeping to stripe pat, sk first 10 (10, 15, 15) sts, join next color with a sc in next st, work across to within last 10 (10, 15, 15) sts. Join next color, ch 1, turn—46 (52, 52, 56) sts. Work even until piece measures 12 (13, 14, 15)"/30.5 (33, 35.5, 38)cm from beg. Fasten off.

FRONT

With A, ch 47 (53, 53, 57). **Foundation row** Sc in 2nd ch from hook and in ch across—46 (52, 52, 56) sts. Ch 1, turn. Cont in pat st.

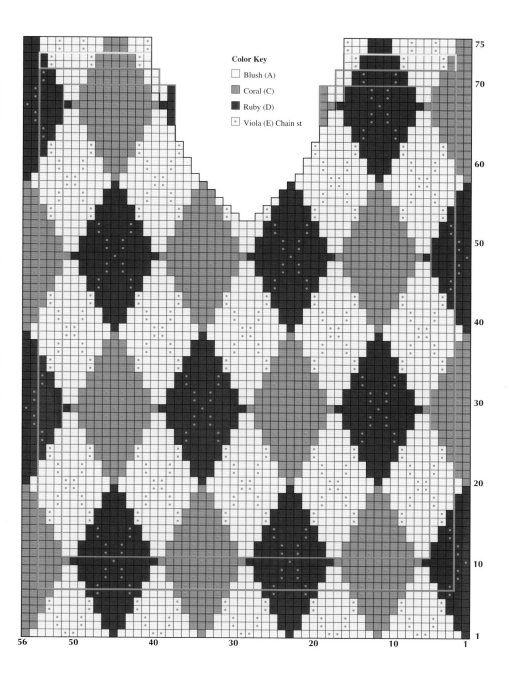

Color Key

- ☐ Blush (A)
- ▨ Coral (C)
- ■ Ruby (D)
- ⬚ Viola (E) Chain st

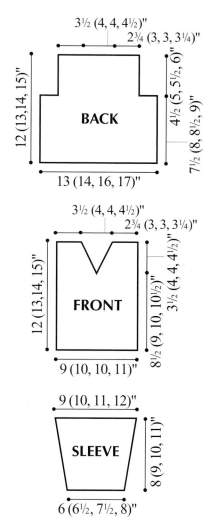

3½ (4, 4, 4½)"

2¾ (3, 3, 3¼)"

12 (13,14, 15)"

BACK

4½ (5, 5½, 6)"

7½ (8, 8½, 9)"

13 (14, 16, 17)"

3½ (4, 4, 4½)"

2¾ (3, 3, 3¼)"

12 (13,14, 15)"

FRONT

3½ (4, 4, 4½)"

8½ (9, 10, 10½)"

9 (10, 10, 11)"

9 (10, 11, 12)"

SLEEVE

8 (9, 10, 11)"

6 (6½, 7½, 8)"

pretty in pink

Beg chart

Row 11 (7, 7, 1) Beg with st 6 (3, 3, 1) and work to st 51 (54, 54, 56). Cont to foll chart in this way until row 52 is completed.

Left neck shaping

Row 53 (RS) Work across first 22 (25, 25, 27) sts, ch 1 turn. Dec 1 st from neck edge every row 6 times, every other row 2 (4, 4, 5) times—14 (15, 15, 16) sts. Work even

until row 69 (71, 73, 75) is completed. Fasten off.

Right neck shaping

Row 53 (RS) Keeping to chart pat, sk 2 center sts, join yarn with a sc in next st, work to end. Cont to work as for left neck, reversing shaping.

SLEEVES

With A, ch 30 (34, 38, 40). **Foundation**

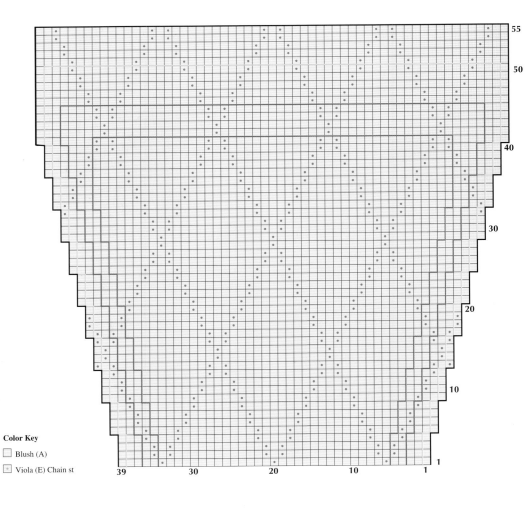

Color Key

☐ Blush (A)

⊡ Viola (E) Chain st

row Sc in 2nd ch from hook and in each ch across—29 (33, 37, 39) sts. Ch 1, turn. Cont in pat st, AT SAME TIME, inc 1 st each side every 4th row 8 (10, 10, 10) times—45 (53, 57, 59) sts. Work even until piece measures 8 (9, 10, 11)"/20 (23, 25.5, 28)cm from beg. Fasten off.

FINISHING

Embroidery
Referring to chart for front, use E to embroider chain-stitch diagonal lines. Referring to chart for sleeves, use B to embroider chain-stitch diagonal lines.

Bobbles
Make 10 (18, 18, 18). With D, ch 2 leaving a long tail for sewing. **Row 1** In 2nd ch from hook work [yo, draw up a lp, yo, draw through 2 lps on hook] 4 times, yo and draw through all 5 lps on hook. Fasten off leaving a long tail for sewing. On each sleeve, sew a bobble where diagonal lines intersect. Sew shoulder and side seams. Set in sleeves, sewing last 1(1, 1½, 1½)"/2.5 (2.5, 4, 4)cm at top of sleeve to armhole sts. Sew sleeve seams.

Neck edging
From RS, join A with a sl st in left shoulder seam. **Rnd 1** Ch 1, making sure that work lies flat, sc around neck edge, dec 1 st over 2 sts at beg of neck shaping. Join rnd with a sl st in ch-1. Fasten off.

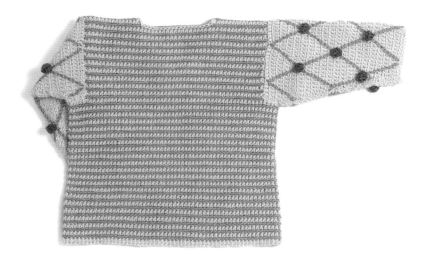

SIZES

Instructions are written for size 6-12 months. Changes for size 18 months-3 years are in parentheses.

FINISHED MEASUREMENTS

Hat
• Circumference 16 (19)"/40.5 (48)cm
Scarf
• 4" x 32" (4" x 36")/10 x 81 (10 x 91.5)cm

MATERIALS

• 1 1¾oz/50g ball (each approx 138yd/ 126m) of Classic Elite Yarns Waterspun (wool ④) in #5036 lime green (A), #5046 teal blue (B), #5027 red purple (C), #5068 orange (D), #5049 blue (F) and #5035 olive green (E)
• Size H/8 (5mm) crochet hook or size to obtain gauges
• Five bobbins

GAUGES

• 16 sts and 16 rows to 4"/10cm over pat st 1 using size H/8 (5mm) hook.
• 16 sts and 12 rows to 4"/10cm over pat st 2 using size H/8 (5mm) hook.
Take time to check gauges.

NOTES

1 See page 131 for working color changes for argyle patterns.
2 Wind A onto 3 bobbins, and B and C onto separate bobbins.
3 See page 131 for working color changes for rows.
4 See page 133 for embroidering chain-stitch.

PATTERN STITCH 1

Row 1 Sc in back lp of each st across. Ch 1, turn.
Rep row 1 for pat st 1.

PATTERN STITCH 2

Row 1 Hdc in back lp of each st across. Ch 2, turn.
Rep row 1 for pat st 2.

STRIPE PATTERN

Working in pat st 2, work 1 row each D, F, A, E, B and C.
Rep these 6 rows for stripe pat.

HAT

FRONT

With A, ch 33 (39). **Foundation row (RS)** Sc in 2nd ch from hook and in each ch across—32 (38) sts. Ch 1, turn. Cont in pat st 1.
Beg chart
Row 3 (1) Beg with st 4 (1) and work to st 35 (38). Cont to foll chart in this way until row 28 (30) is completed. Fasten off.

BACK

With B, ch 33 (39). **Foundation row** Sc in 2nd ch from hook and in each ch across— 32 (38) sts. Ch 1, turn. Cont in pat st 1 and work even until piece measure same length as front. Fasten off.

FINISHING

Embroidery
Referring to chart, use D to embroider

chain-stitch diagonal lines on front. Referring to same chart, use F to embroider chain-stitch diagonal lines on back. Place front and back tog, WS facing. With front facing you, use D to sc pieces tog working 3 sc in each corner. Fasten off.

Edging
From RS, join C with a sl st in side seam. **Rnd 1** Ch 1, sc in each st around—66 (78) sts. Join rnd with a sl st in ch-1changing to D. **Rnd 2** Ch 1, sc in back lp of each st around. Join rnd with a sl st in ch-1 changing to F. **Rnd 3** Rep rnd 2, changing to B. **Rnd 4** Rep rnd 2. Fasten off.

Pompoms
(make 2)
Using all colors, make a 2"/5cm in diameter pompom (see pompom instructions). Sew a pompom to each corner of hat.

SCARF
Beg at side edge with C, ch 130 (156). **Foundation row** Hdc in 3rd ch from hook and in each ch across—128 (154) sts. Join D, ch 2, turn. Cont in pat st 2 and stripe pat and work even until piece measures 4"/10cm from beg. Fasten off.

FINISHING
Pompoms
(make 6)
Using all colors, make a 1½"/4cm in diameter pompom (see pompom instructions). Sew 3 pompoms across each end of scarf.

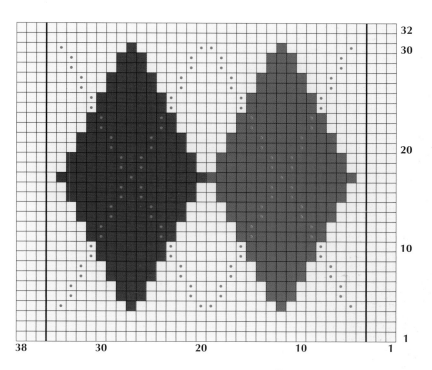

Color Key
☐ Lime (A)
▦ Teal blue (B)
■ Red purple (C)
⊡ Orange (D) chain st

c r o s s   m y   h e a r t

SIZES

Instructions are written for size 3-6 months. Changes for sizes 9-12 months, 18-24 months and 3 years are in parentheses.

FINISHED MEASUREMENTS

- Chest 18 (20, 22, 24)"/45.5 (51, 56, 61)cm
- Length 14 (15, 17, 18)"/35.5 (38, 43, 45.5)cm

MATERIALS

- 3 (4, 4, 5) 1¾oz/50g balls (approx 136yd/124m) of Patons Grace (cotton ③) in #60724 teal (MC)
- 1 ball each in #60723 aqua (A) and #60711 apple (B)
- Size G/6 (4mm) crochet hook or size to obtain gauge
- Eleven bobbins
- Small safety pin
- 1½yd/1.5m of ¼"/6mm apple green satin ribbon

GAUGE

20 sts and 20 rows to 4"/10cm over pat st using size G/6 (4mm) hook.
Take time to check gauge.

NOTES

1 Front and back are made separately, then sewn tog.
2 Skirt is made in one piece from bodice to hem.
3 See page 131 for working color changes for argyle patterns.
4 Wind MC onto 5 bobbins and A and B onto 3 bobbins each.
5 See page 133 for embroidering chain-stitch.

PATTERN STITCH 1

Row 1 Sc in back lp of each st across. Ch 1, turn.
Rep row 1 for pat st 1.

PATTERN STITCH 2

Rnd 1 Ch 1, sc in back lp of each st around. Join rnd with a sl st in ch-1.
Rep rnd 1 for pat st 2.

BACK BODICE

With MC, ch 47 (51, 57, 61). **Foundation row** Sc in 2nd ch from hook and in each ch across—46 (50, 56, 60) sts. Ch 1, turn. Cont in pat st 1.

Beg chart 1 (1, 2, 2)

Row 1 Beg with st 3 (1, 3, 1) and work to st 48 (50, 58, 60). Cont to foll chart in this way until row 10 (10, 16, 16) is completed. Fasten off. Turn work.

Armhole shaping

Row 11 (11, 17, 17) Keeping to chart pat, sk first 3 (3, 4, 4) sts, join yarn with a sc in next st, work across to within last 3 (3, 4, 4) sts. Ch 1, turn—40 (44, 48, 52) sts. Dec 1 st each side every row 2 (2, 3, 3) times—36 (40, 42, 46) sts. Work even until row 16 (16, 20, 20) is completed. Ch 1, turn.

Left neck shaping

Row 17 (17, 21, 21) Work across first 14 (16, 17, 19) sts, ch 1 turn. Dec 1 st from neck edge every row 4 (5, 3, 3) times, every other row 0 (0, 2, 3) times—10 (11, 12, 13) sts. Work even until row 26 (28, 36, 38) is completed. Fasten off.

Right neck shaping

Row 17 (17, 21, 21) Keeping to chart pat, sk 8 center sts, join yarn with a sc in next st, work to end. Cont to work as for left neck, reversing shaping.

FRONT BODICE

Work as for back bodice.

Embroidery

Referring to chart (1, 1, 2, 2), use MC and B to embroider chain-stitch diagonal lines on back and front. Sew shoulder and side seams.

SKIRT

With RS facing, join MC with a sl st in left side seam. **Foundation rnd** Ch 1, working in bottom lps of foundation ch, work 2 sc in each bottom lp around—92 (100, 112, 120) sts. Mark last st made with the safety

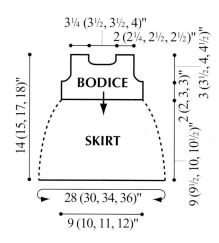

pin to indicate end of rnd. Join rnd with a sl st in ch-1. **Inc rnd** *Working through back lps, work 2 sc in next st, sc in next st; rep from * around—138 (150, 168, 180) sts. Join rnd with a sl st in ch-1. Cont in pat st 2 and work even until skirt measures 9 (9½, 10, 10½)"/23 (24, 25.5, 26.5)cm from beg.

Edging

Rnd 1 Ch 1, *sc in next st, ch 2, sk next st; rep from * around. Join rnd with a sl st in ch-1. Fasten off.

FINISHING

Neck edging

From RS, join MC with a sl st in left shoulder seam. **Rnd 1** Ch 1, making sure that work lies flat, sc around neck edge. Join rnd with a sl st in ch-1. Fasten off. Rep edging around each armhole. Beg and ending at center front, weave ribbon under and over sts of first rnd between bodice and skirt.

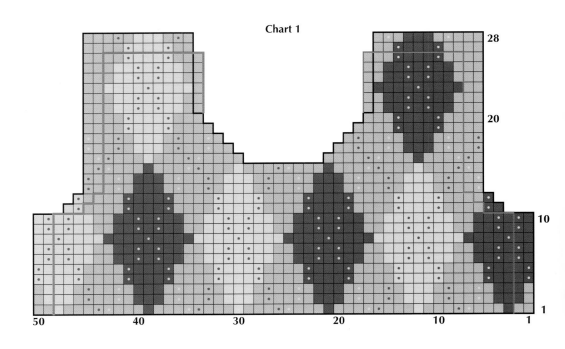

Chart 1

Chart 2

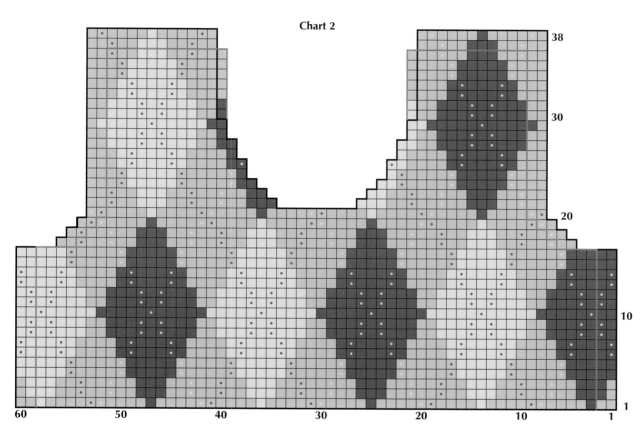

Color Key

■ Teal (MC)

■ Aqua (A)

□ Apple (B)

⊡ Teal (MC) Chain st

□ Apple (B) Chain st

h i g h l a n d   c h a r m

SIZES

Instructions are written for size 3-6 months. Changes for sizes 9-12 months, 18-24 months and 3 years are in parentheses.

FINISHED MEASUREMENTS

- Chest (buttoned) 22 (24, 26, 28)"/56 (61, 66, 71)cm
- Length 12 (13, 14, 15)"/30.5 (33, 35.5, 38)cm
- Upper arm 9 (10, 11, 12)"/23 (25.5, 28, 30.5)cm

MATERIALS

- 2 1¾oz/50g balls (each approx 138yd/ 126m) of Classic Elite Yarns Waterspun (wool ④) in #5036 lime green (A)
- 1 ball each in #5049 blue (B), #5035 olive green (C), #5046 teal blue (D), #5027 red purple (E) and #5068 orange (F)
- Size H/8 (5mm) crochet hook or size to obtain gauge
- Nine bobbins
- 4 (4, 5, 5) ¾"/19mm buttons

GAUGE

16 sts and 16 rows to 4"/10cm over pat st using size H/8 (5mm) hook.
Take time to check gauge.

NOTES

1 See page 131 for working color changes for argyle patterns.

2 Wind A onto 2 bobbins and B, C, D and E onto separate bobbins.

3 See page 131 for working color changes for rows.

4 See page 133 for embroidering chain-stitch.

PATTERN STITCH

Row 1 Sc in back lp of each st across. Ch 1, turn.
Rep row 1 for pat st.

STRIPE PATTERN

Working in pat st, work 1 row each B, C, D, E, F and A.
Rep these 6 rows for stripe pat.

BACK

With A, ch 53 (57, 65, 69). **Foundation row** Sc in 2nd ch from hook and in each ch across—52 (56, 64, 68) sts. Join B, ch 1, turn. Cont in pat st and stripe pat and work even until piece measures 7½ (8, 8½, 9)"/19 (20, 21.5, 23)cm from beg. Fasten off. Turn work.

Armhole shaping

Next row Keeping to stripe pat, sk first 8 (8, 12, 12) sts, join next color with a sc in next st, work across to within last 8 (8, 12, 12) sts. Join next color, ch 1, turn—36 (40, 40, 44) sts. Work even until piece measures 12 (13, 14,15)"/30.5 (33, 35.5, 38)cm from beg. Fasten off.

LEFT FRONT

With A, ch 18 (20, 20, 22). **Foundation row (WS)** Sc in 2nd ch from hook and in each ch across—17 (19, 19, 21) sts. Ch 1, turn. Cont in pat st.

Beg chart 1

Row 7 (5, 3, 1) Beg with st 3 (2, 2, 1) and work to st 19 (20, 20, 21). Cont to foll chart in this way until row 40 is completed.

Neck shaping

Row 41 (RS) Work across to within last 2 sts, dec 1 st over last 2 sts. Cont to dec 1 st from neck edge every row 3 (4, 4, 5) times more, every other row 4 times—9 (10, 10, 11) sts. Work even until row 54 (56, 58, 60) is completed. Fasten off.

RIGHT FRONT

Work as for left front, foll chart 2 and reversing neck shaping.

LEFT SLEEVE

With E, ch 25 (29, 31, 33). **Foundation row** Sc in 2nd ch from hook and in each ch across—24 (28, 30, 32) sts. Cont in pat st and inc 1 st each side every 4th row 6 (6, 7, 8) times—36 (40, 44, 48) sts. Work even until piece measures 8 (9, 10, 11)"/20 (23, 25.5, 28)cm from beg. Fasten off.

RIGHT SLEEVE

Work as for left sleeve using B.

FINISHING

Embroidery

Referring to charts 1 and 2, use F to embroider chain-stitch diagonal lines on fronts. Referring to chart 3, use A to embroider chain-stitch diagonal lines on sleeves. Sew shoulder and side seams. Set in sleeves, sewing last 1 (1, 1½, 1½)"/2.5 (2.5, 4, 4)cm at top of sleeve to armhole sts. Sew sleeve seams.

Edging

From RS, join F with a sl st in left side seam. **Rnd 1** Ch 1, making sure that work lies flat, sc around entire edge, working 3 sc in each corner. Join rnd with a sl st in ch-1. Fasten off.

Buttonband

With RS facing and F, join yarn with a sc in first st at bottom edge of right front. Sc in each st to beg of neck shaping. Ch 1, turn. Work 1 row even. Fasten off. Place markers on band for 4 (4, 5, 5) buttons, with the first ¾"/2cm from beg of neck shaping, the last 1¼"/3cm from bottom edge and the rest spaced evenly between.

Buttonhole band

With RS facing and F, join yarn with a sc in first st at beg of neck shaping of left front. **Buttonhole row** *Sc to marker, ch 2, sk next 2 sts; rep from * to first st at bottom edge. Ch 1, turn. **Next row** Sc in each st and work 2 sc in each ch-2 sp across. Fasten off. Sew on buttons.

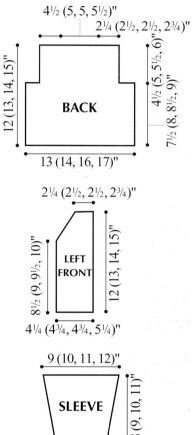

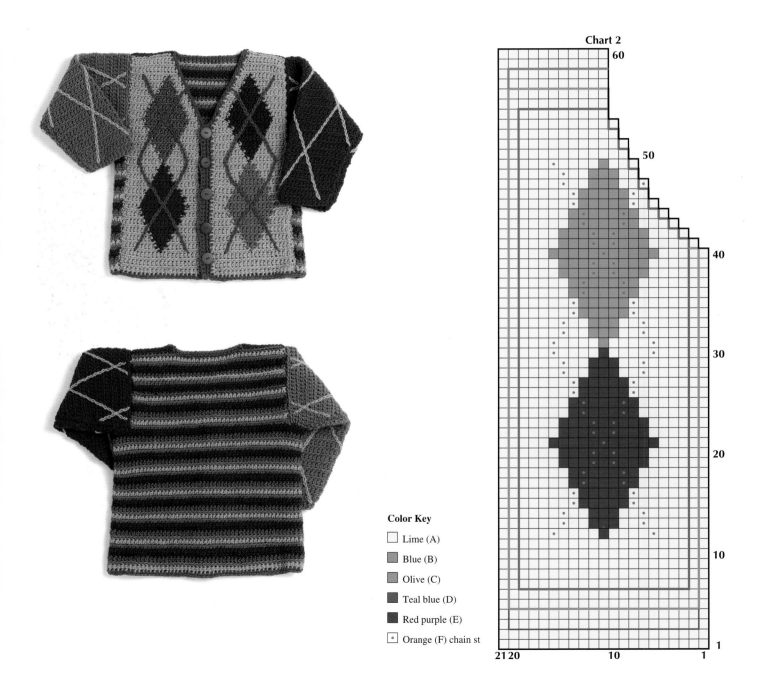

Chart 2

Color Key

☐ Lime (A)

▨ Blue (B)

▨ Olive (C)

▨ Teal blue (D)

■ Red purple (E)

⊡ Orange (F) chain st

Chart 1

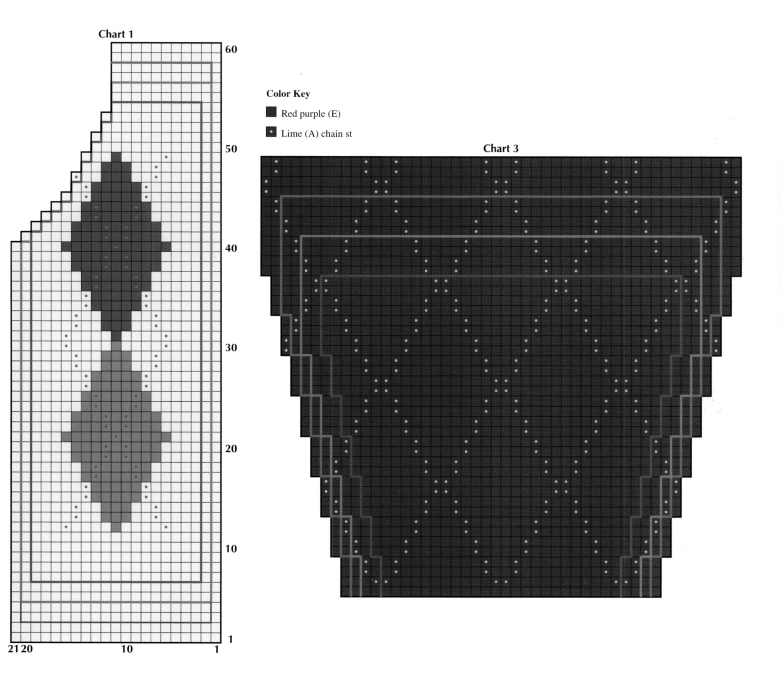

Color Key
- ■ Red purple (E)
- ▨ Lime (A) chain st

Chart 3

FINISHED MEASUREMENTS

• 27" x 33"/68.5 x 84cm

MATERIALS

• 6 1¾oz/50g hanks (each approx 108yd/99m) of Tahki Yarns/Tahki•Stacy Charles, Inc. Cotton Classic (cotton ⑤) in #3446 light pink (MC)
• 1 hank each in #3463 dark pink (A), #3475 coral (B) and #3418 burgundy (C)
• Size I/9 (5.5mm) crochet hook or size to obtain gauge

GAUGE

16 sts and 12 rows to 4"/10cm over pat st using size I/9 (5.5mm) hook.
Take time to check gauge.

NOTES

1 See page 131 for working color changes for argyle patterns.
2 See page 133 for embroidering chain-stitch.

PATTERN STITCH

Row 1 Hdc in back lp of each st across.
Ch 2, turn.
Rep row 1 for pat st.

BLANKET

With MC, ch 110. **Foundation row** Hdc in 3rd ch from hook and in each ch across—108 sts. Ch 2, turn. Cont in pat st and work even until piece measures 2½"/6cm from beg.

Beg chart

Row 1 (RS) With MC, work across first 12 sts, beg chart with st 1 and work to st 84, with MC, work across last 12 sts. Ch 2, turn. Cont to foll chart in this way to row 84. With MC, work even for 2½"/6cm. Ch 1, turn to side edge.

Edging

Rnd 1 Making sure that work lies flat, sc around entire edge, working 3 sc in each corner. Join rnd with a sl st in ch-1. Fasten off.

FINISHING

Embroidery

Referring to chart, use C to embroider chain-stitch diagonal lines.

Color Key

■ Lt pink (MC)
■ Dk pink (A)
■ Coral (B)
• Burgundy (C) Chain st

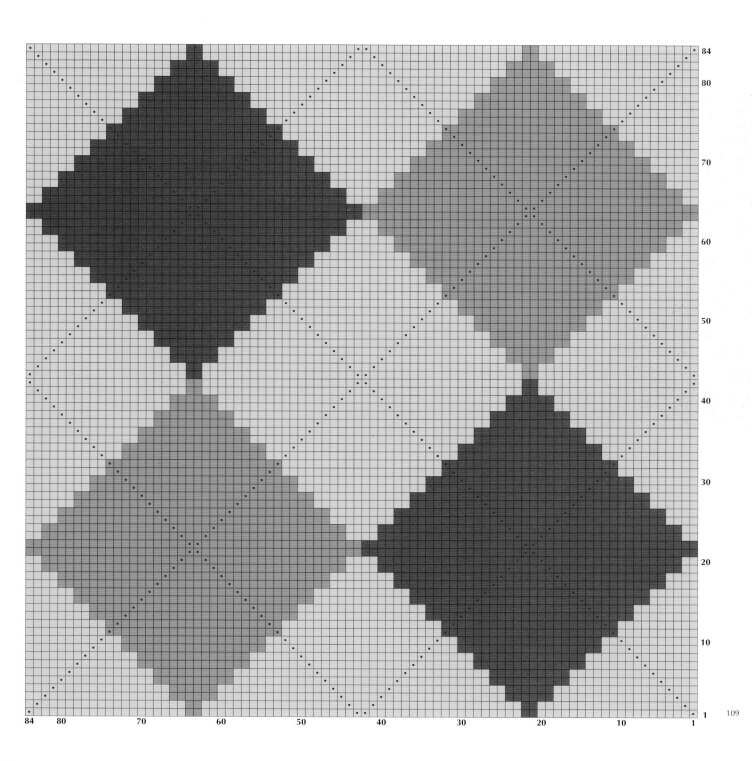

84
80

70

60

50

40

30

20

10

1

84 80   70   60   50   40   30   20   10   1

b e r r y   p r e t t y

SIZES

Instructions are written for size 3-6 months. Changes for sizes 9-12 months, 18-24 months and 3 years are in parentheses.

FINISHED MEASUREMENTS

* Chest 22 (24, 26, 28)"/56 (61, 66, 71)cm
* Length 11 (12, 13, 14)"/28 (30.5, 33, 35.5)cm
* Upper arm 9 (10, 11, 12)"/23 (25.5, 28, 30.5)cm

MATERIALS

* *3 (4, 4, 5) 3½oz/100g hanks (each approx 150yd/137m) of Knit One, Crochet Too Tartelette (cotton/nylon ⑥) in #235 raspberry*
* *Size J/10 (6mm) crochet hook or size to obtain gauge*
* *1 set of markers*

GAUGE

11 sts and 8 rows to 4"/10cm over hdc using size J/10 (6mm) hook.
Take time to check gauge.

BACK

Ch 32 (36, 38, 40). **Row 1 (WS)** Hdc in 3rd ch from hook and in each ch across—30 (34, 36, 38) sts. Ch 2, turn. **Row 2** Hdc in each st across. Ch 2, turn. Rep row 2 for pat st and work even until piece measures 11 (12, 13, 14)"/28 (30.5, 33, 35.5)cm from beg. Fasten off.

FRONT

Work as for back until piece measures 7½ (8, 8½, 9)"/19 (20, 21.5, 23)cm from beg, end with a WS row.
Left neck shaping
Next row (RS) Work across first 14 (16, 17, 18) sts, ch 2, turn. Dec 1 st from neck edge on next row, then every other row 3 (4, 4, 5) times more—10 (11, 12, 12) sts. Work even until piece measures same length as back. Fasten off.
Right neck shaping
Next row (RS) Sk 2 center sts, join yarn with an hdc in next st, work to end—14 (16, 17, 18) sts. Ch 2, turn. Cont to work as for left neck, reversing shaping.

SLEEVES

Ch 22 (24, 27, 29). **Row 1 (WS)** Hdc in 3rd ch from hook and in each ch across—20 (22, 25, 27) sts. Ch 2, turn. **Row 2** Hdc in each st across. Ch 2, turn. Rep row 2 for pat st and work even until piece measures 1 (1, 2, 2)"/2.5 (2.5, 5, 5)cm from beg. Inc 1 st each side every other row 3 times—26 (28, 31, 33) sts. Work even until piece measures 4 (5, 6, 7)"/10 (12.7, 15, 17.5)cm from beg. Fasten off.

COLLAR
(make 2 pieces)
Ch 15 (17, 19, 21). **Row 1 (WS)** Sc in 2nd ch from hook and in each ch across— 14 (16, 18, 20) sts. Ch 2, turn. **Row 2** Hdc in each st across. Ch 2, turn. Rep row 2 for pat st and inc 1 st each side every row 2 (3, 3, 4) times—18 (22, 24, 28) sts. Ch 3, turn.

Edging
Next row *Sk next st, work (dc, tr, dc) in next st, sk next st, sc in next st; rep from *

to end of row, then cont along side edge (front edge of collar) to row 1. Fasten off.

FINISHING
Sew shoulder seams. Place markers 4½ (5, 5½, 6)"/11.5 (12.5, 14, 15)cm down from shoulder seams on front and back. Sew sleeves to armholes between markers. Sew side and sleeve seams. Sew on collar pieces.

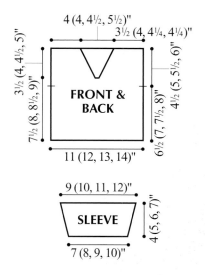

SIZES

Instructions are written for size 12 months. Changes for sizes 24 months and 3 years are in parentheses.

FINISHED MEASUREMENTS

• Chest (buttoned) 24 (26, 28)"/61 (66, 71)cm
• Length 16 (19, 21)"/40.5 (48, 53)cm
• Upper arm 10 (12, 13)"/25.5 (30.5, 33)cm

MATERIALS

• 3 (4, 5) 5oz/140g skeins (each approx 253yd/231m) of Red Heart/Coats & Clark TLC (acrylic ⑤) in #5745 medium pink (MC)
• 4 (5, 6) 3½oz/100g hanks (each approx 150yd/137m) of Friends, Inc. Mustaciao (acrylic ⑥) in off white (CC)
• Size H/8 and I/9 (5 and 5.5mm) crochet hooks or sizes to obtain gauges
• Four ¾"/19mm buttons
• 1 set of markers

GAUGES

14 sts and 10 rows to 4"/10cm over pat st using size H/8 (5mm) hook and MC.
11 sts and 10 rows to 4"/10cm over sc using size I/9 (5.5mm) hook and CC. Take time to check gauges.

NOTE

It is sometimes difficult seeing the sts when working with furry yarn. For best results, count sts as you work across each row to make sure you do not skip or miss a st.

PATTERN STITCH

(over an even number of sts)
Row 1 *Hdc into front lp of next st, hdc into back lp of next st; rep from * across. Ch 2, turn.
Rep row 1 for pat st.

BACK

With smaller hook and MC, ch 57 (65, 71). **Foundation row** Sc in 2nd ch from hook and in each ch across—56 (64, 70) sts. Ch 2, turn. Cont in pat st and work even for 1"/2.5cm. Keeping to pat st, dec 1 st each side every 4th row 7 (9, 10) times—42 (46, 50) sts. Work even until piece measures 11 (13, 14½)"/28 (33, 37)cm from beg. Do not ch, turn.

Armhole shaping

Next row Sl st across first 4 sts, ch 2, work across to within last 4 sts, ch 2, turn—34 (38, 42) sts. Work even until armhole measures 4½ (5½, 6)"/11.5 (14, 15)cm.

Right shoulder

Next row Work across first 10 (10, 12) sts. Ch 2, turn. Work even for 1 row. Fasten off.

Left shoulder

Next row Sk 14 (18, 18) center sts, join yarn with a hdc in next st, work to end. Work even for 1 more row. Fasten off.

LEFT FRONT

With smaller hook and MC, ch 29 (33, 37). **Foundation row** Sc in 2nd ch from hook and in each ch across—28 (32, 36) sts. Ch 2, turn. Cont in pat st and work even for 1"/2.5cm, end with a WS row. Keeping to pat st, dec 1 st at beg of next row, then at same edge every 4th row 6 (8, 9) times more—21 (23, 26) sts. Work even until piece measures 11 (13, 14½)"/28 (33, 37)cm from beg, end with a WS row. Do not ch, turn.

Armhole shaping

Next row (RS) Sl st across first 4 sts, ch 2, work to end—17 (19, 22) sts. Work even until armhole measures 3 (3½, 3½)"/7.5 (9, 9)cm from beg, end with a WS row.

Neck shaping

Next row (RS) Work across to within last 4 (4, 5) sts. Ch 2, turn. Dec 1 st from neck edge every row 3 (5, 5) times—10 (10, 12) sts. Work even until piece measures same length as back. Fasten off.

RIGHT FRONT

Work as for left front reversing shaping.

SLEEVES

With smaller hook and MC, ch 25 (27, 29). **Foundation row** Sc in 2nd ch from hook and in each ch across—24 (26, 28) sts. Ch 2, turn. Cont in pat st and work even for 1"/2.5cm. Keeping to pat st, inc 1 st each side every other row 3 (5, 6) times, every 4th row 3 times—36 (42, 46) sts. Work even until piece measures 9 (10, 11)"/23 (25.5, 28)cm from beg. Fasten off.

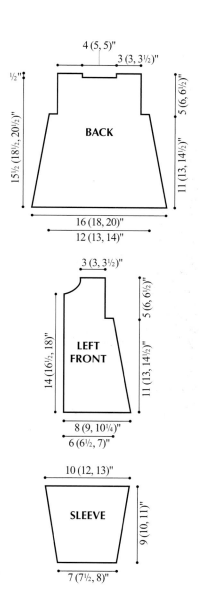

COLLAR

With larger hook and CC, ch 31 (39, 43).
Foundation row Sc in 2nd ch from hook and in each ch across—30 (38, 42) sts. Ch 1, turn.

Row 1 Sc in first st, inc in next st, sc in next 2 sts, inc in next st, sc in next 5 (7, 9) sts, inc in next st, sc in next 8 (12, 12) sts, inc in next st, sc in next 5 (7, 9) sts, inc in next st, sc in next 2 sts, inc in next st, sc in last st—36 (44, 48) sts. Ch 1, turn.

Row 2 Sc in first st, inc in next st, sc in next 3 sts, inc in next st, sc in next 6 (8, 10) sts, inc in next st, sc in next 10 (14, 14) sts, inc in next st, sc in next 6 (8, 10) sts, inc in next st, sc in next 3 sts, inc in next st, sc in last st—42 (50, 54) sts. Ch 1, turn.

Row 3 Sc in first st, inc in next st, sc in next 4 sts, inc in next st, sc in next 7 (9, 11) sts, inc in next st, sc in next 12 (16, 16) sts, inc in next st, sc in next 7 (9, 11) sts, inc in next st, sc in next 4 sts, inc in next st, sc in last st—48 (56, 60) sts. Ch 1, turn.

Row 4 Sc in first st, inc in next st, sc in next 5 sts, inc in next st, sc in next 8 (10, 12) sts, inc in next st, sc in next 14 (18, 18) sts, inc in next st, sc in next 8 (10, 12) sts, inc in next st, sc in next 5 sts, inc in next st, sc in last st—54 (62, 66) sts. Ch 1, turn.

Row 5 Sc in first st, inc in next st, sc in next 6 sts, inc in next st, sc in next 9 (11, 13) sts, inc in next st, sc in next 16 (20, 20) sts, inc in next st, sc in next 9 (11, 13) sts, inc in next st, sc in next 6 sts, inc in next st, sc in last st—60 (68, 72) sts. Ch 1, turn.

Row 6 Sc in first st, inc in next st, sc in next 7 sts, inc in next st, sc in next 10 (12, 14) sts, inc in next st, sc in next 18 (22, 22) sts, inc in next st, sc in next 10 (12, 14) sts, inc in next st, sc in next 7 sts, inc in next st, sc in last st—66 (74, 78) sts. Ch 1, turn. Work 1 row even. Fasten off.

CUFFS

With larger hook and CC, ch 21 (23, 25).
Foundation row Sc in 2nd ch from hook and in each ch across—20 (22, 24) sts. Ch 1, turn. Work even in sc for 2 rows. **Inc row** Sc in first st, inc in next st, sc in each st to within last 2 sts, inc in next st, sc in

last st—22 (24, 26) sts. Ch 1, turn. Work 1 row even. Ch 1, turn. Rep last 2 rows once more—24 (26, 28) sts. Fasten off.

FINISHING

Sew shoulder seams.

Buttonband

With RS facing, smaller hook and MC, work 1 row of sc evenly along left front edge. Ch 1, turn. Work 2 rows even. Fasten off. Place markers on band for 4 buttons, with the first 1"/2.5cm from neck edge and the others spaced 2"/5cm apart.

Buttonhole band

Work as for buttonband until 1 row has been completed. **Buttonhole row** *Sc to marker, ch 2, sk next 2 sts; rep from * to end. Ch 1, turn. **Next row** Sc in each st and work 2 sc in each ch-2 sp across. Fasten off. Set in sleeves, sewing last 1"/2.5cm at top of sleeve to armhole sts. Sew side and sleeve seams. Sew on collar and cuffs. Sew on buttons.

p a t t e r n   p l a y

SIZES

Instructions are written for size 6-12 months. Changes for size 18 months-3 years are in parentheses.

FINISHED MEASUREMENTS

- Chest 23½ (27)"/59.5 (68.5)cm
- Length 12 (14)"/30.5 (35.5)cm

MATERIALS

- 1 1¾oz/50g balls (each approx 128yd/117m) of Patons Country Garden DK (wool ③) each in #43 cedar green (A), #38 sea green (B), #32 delphinium (C), #30 blue smoke (D) and #37 shutter green (E)
- Size G/6 (4mm) crochet hook or size to obtain gauge

GAUGE

18 sts and 18 rows to 4"/10cm over sc using size G/6 (4mm) hook.
Take time to check gauge.

NOTE

See page 131 for making color changes.

PATTERN STITCH

Row 1 (WS) Sc in each st across. Join B, ch 3, turn.

Row 2 Dc in first st, *dc between next 2 sts of row below, dc in next st; rep from * to end. Join C, ch 1, turn.

Row 3 Sc in front lps of first 2 sts, *in next st work [yo, draw up a lp, yo, draw through 2 lps on hook] 3 times, yo and draw through all 4 lps on hook (bobble made), sc in front lps of next 3 sts; rep from *, end bobble in next st, sc in front lps of last 2 sts. Join D, ch 1, turn.

Row 4 Sc in each st across. Ch 1, turn.

Row 5 Sc in front lp of each st across. Join E, ch 1, turn.

Row 6 Sc in first st, sk next st, *work 3 dc in next st (shell made), sk next st, sc in next st, sk next st; rep from *, end work 3 dc in next st (shell made), sk next st, sc in last st. Join B, ch 3, turn.

Row 7 Work 2 dc in first sc (half shell made), *work 3 dc in next sc, sc in 3rd dc of next shell; rep from *, end work 2 dc in last sc. Join C, ch 2, turn.

Row 8 Sc in each sc and dc across. Ch 1, turn.

Row 9 Sc in front lp of each st across. Join A, ch 3, turn.

Row 10 Rep row 2. Join B, ch 1, turn.

Row 11 Rep row 3. Join D, ch 1, turn.

Row 12 Rep row 1. Join E, ch 3, turn.

Row 13 Rep row 2. Join C, ch 1, turn.

Row 14 Rep row 6. Join D, ch 3, turn.

Row 15 Rep row 7. Join A, ch 1, turn.

Row 16 Rep row 1. Ch 1, turn.

Rep rows 1-16 for pat st.

BACK

With A, ch 54 (62). **Foundation row (RS)** Sc in 2nd ch from hook and in each ch across—53 (61) sts. Ch 1, turn. Cont in pat st and work even until piece measures 7½ (8½)"/19 (21.5)cm from beg, end ready for row 12 (16). Fasten off. Turn work.

Armhole shaping

Next row (RS) Sk first 4 sts, join D (A) with a sc in next st, work across to within last 4 sts, keeping to pat st, ch and turn—45 (53) sts. Work even until piece measures 12 (14)"/30.5 (35.5)cm from beg. Fasten off.

FRONT

Work as for back until armhole shaping and 1 row have been completed.

Left neck shaping

Next row Keeping to pat st, work across first 21 (25) sts, ch and turn. Dec 1 st from neck edge every row 9 (10) times—12 (15) sts. Work even until piece measures same

length as back. Fasten off.

Right neck shaping

Next row Keeping to pat st, sk 3 center sts, join yarn in next st, work to end. Cont to work as for left neck, reversing shaping.

FINISHING

Sew shoulder and side seams.

Neck edging

From RS, join A with a sl st in left shoulder seam. **Rnd 1** Ch 1, making sure that work lies flat, sc around neck edge. Join rnd with a sl st in ch-1. Fasten off. Rep edging around each armhole.

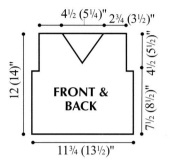

4½ (5¼)" 2¾ (3½)"

12 (14)"

4½ (5½)"

FRONT & BACK

7½ (8½)"

11¾ (13½)"

h i p p i e   c h i c

SIZES

Instructions are written for size 6-12 months. Changes for size 18 months-3 years are in parentheses.

FINISHED MEASUREMENTS

- Chest (closed) 25 (29)"/63.5 (73.5)cm
- Length 13½ (16)"/34 (40.5)cm

MATERIALS

- *2 1¾oz/50g balls (each approx 128yd/117m) of Patons Country Garden DK (wool ③) in #51 chocolate (A)*
- *1 ball each in #77 natural (B), #25 beetroot (C) and #28 wild violet (D)*
- *1 3½oz/100g hank (approx 150yd/137m) of Friends, Inc. Mustaciao (acrylic ⑥) in chocolate (E)*
- *Size G/6 and I/9 (4 and 5.5mm) crochet hooks or sizes to obtain gauges*

GAUGES

- 18 sts and 16 rows to 4"/10cm over hdc using size G/6 (4mm) hook and A.
- 11 sts and 10 rows to 4"/10cm over sc using size I/9 (5.5mm) hook and E.
Take time to check gauges.

NOTES

1 See page 131 for making color changes.
2 It is sometimes difficult seeing the sts when working with furry yarn. For best results, count sts as you work across each row to make sure you do not skip or miss a st.

PATTERN STITCH

Row 1 (WS) Sc in first st, sk next st, *work 3 dc in next st (shell made), sk next st, sc in next st, sk next st; rep from *, end work 3 dc in next st (shell), sk next st, sc in last st. Join C, ch 3, turn.

Row 2 Work 2 dc in first sc (half shell made), *work 3 dc in next sc, sc in 3rd dc of next shell; rep from *, end work 2 dc in last sc. Join D, ch 1, turn.

Row 3 Sc in first 2 sts, *in next st work [yo, draw up a lp, yo, draw through 2 lps on hook] 3 times, yo and draw through all 4 lps on hook (bobble made), sc in next 3 sts; rep from *, end bobble in next st, sc in last 2 sts. Join A, ch 2, turn.

Rows 4 and 5 Hdc in each st across. After row 5 is completed, join B, ch 3, turn.

Row 6 Dc in first st, *dc between next 2 sts of row below, dc in next st; rep from * to end. Join C, ch 1, turn.

Row 7 Rep row 1. Join D, ch 3, turn.

Row 8 Rep row 2. Join A, ch 1, turn.

Work rows 1-8 for pat st.

STRIPE PATTERN 1

Row 1 Sc in each st across. Ch 2, turn.

Row 2 Hdc in each st across. Join B, ch 3, turn.

Row 3 Dc in first st, *dc between next 2 sts of row below, dc in next st; rep from * to end. Join C, ch 1, turn.

Row 4 Rep row 1. Join D, ch 1, turn.

Row 5 Rep row 1. Join C, ch 1, turn.

Row 6 Rep row 1. Join B, ch 3, turn.

Row 7 Dc in each st across. Join A, ch 2, turn.

Row 8 Rep row 2. Ch 1, turn.

Rows 9 and 10 Rep row 1. After row 10 is completed, join B, ch 1, turn.

Work rows 1-10 for stripe pat 1.

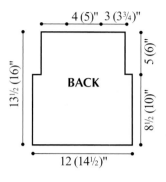

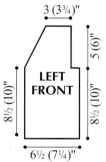

STRIPE PATTERN 2

Row 1 Sc in each st across. Ch 2, turn.

Rows 2-4 Hdc in each st across. After row 4 is completed, join B, ch 3, turn.

Row 5 Dc in first st, *dc between next 2 sts of row below, dc in next st; rep from * to end. Join C, ch 1, turn.

Row 6 Rep row 1. Join D, ch 1, turn.

Row 7 Rep row 1. Join C, ch 1, turn.

Row 8 Rep row 1. Join B, ch 3, turn.

Row 9 Dc in each st across. Join A, ch 2, turn.

Rows 10-12 Rep row 2. After row 12 is completed, ch 1, turn.

Rows 13 and 14 Rep row 1. After row 14 is completed, join B, ch 1, turn.

Work rows 1-14 for stripe pat 2.

BACK

With smaller hook and A, ch 55 (67).

Foundation row (RS) Hdc in 3rd ch from hook and in each ch across—53 (65) sts. Join B, ch 1, turn. Work 8 rows of pat st, 10 (14) rows of stripe pat 1 (2), then 8 rows of pat st. Piece should measure 8½ (10)"/21.5 (25.5)cm from beg. Fasten off. Turn work.

Armhole shaping

Next row (WS) Sk first 4 sts, join A with a sc in next st, work row 1 of stripe pat 1 (2) across to within last 4 sts. Ch 2, turn—45 (57) sts. Work rem 9 (13) rows of stripe pat 1 (2), then work pat st until piece measures 13½ (16)"/34 (40.5)cm from beg. Fasten off.

LEFT FRONT

With smaller hook and A, ch 31 (35).

Foundation row (RS) Hdc in 3rd ch from hook and in each ch across—29 (33) sts. Join B, ch 1, turn. Work 8 rows of pat st, 10 (14) rows of stripe pat 1 (2), then 8 rows of pat st.

Armhole shaping

Next row (WS) Working in stripe pat 1 (2), then pat st, work across to within last 4 sts. Ch 2, turn—25 (29) sts.

Neck shaping

Next row (RS) Work across, dec 1 st over last 2 sts. Cont to dec 1 st from (neck) edge every row 6 times more, every other row 5 times—13 (17) sts. Work even until piece measures same length as back. Fasten off.

RIGHT FRONT

Work as for left front to armhole shaping, then work 1 row of stripe pat 1 (2). Keeping to stripe pat and pat st, cont to work as for left front, reversing shaping.

COLLAR

With larger hook and E, ch 43 (53).

Foundation row Sc in 2nd ch from hook and in each ch across—42 (52) sts. Ch 1, turn. Cont in sc.

Row 1 Dec 1 st over first 2 sts, sc in next 13 (16) sts, work 2 sc in next st, sc in next 10 (14) sts, work 2 sc in next st, sc in next 13 (16) sts, dec 1 st over last 2 sts—42 (52) sts. Ch 1, turn.

Row 2 Dec 1 st over first 2 sts, sc in next 12 (15) sts, [work 2 sc in next st] twice, sc in next 10 (14) sts, [work 2 sc in next st] twice, sc in next 12 (15) sts, dec 1 st over last 2 sts—44 (54) sts. Ch 1, turn.

Row 3 [Dec 1 st over 2 sts] twice, sc in next 11 (14) sts, [work 2 sc in next st] twice, sc in next 10 (14) sts, [work 2 sc in next st] twice, sc in next 11 (14) sts, [dec 1 st over next 2 sts] twice—44 (54) sts. Ch 1, turn.

Row 4 [Dec 1 st over 2 sts] twice, sc in next 36 (46) sts, [dec 1 st over next 2 sts] twice—40 (50) sts. Ch 1, turn.

Rows 5 and 6 Dec 1 st over first 2 sts, sc in next 12 (15) sts, work 2 sc in next st, sc in next 10 (14) sts, work 2 sc in next st, sc in next 12 (15) sts, dec 1 st over last 2 sts—40 (50) sts. Ch 1, turn.

Row 7 [Dec 1 st over 2 sts] twice, sc in next 32 (42) sts, [dec 1 st over next 2 sts] twice—36 (46) sts. Ch 1, turn.

Rows 8 and 9 Sc in each st across. Ch 1, turn. After row 9 is completed, fasten off.

FINISHING

Sew shoulder and side seams.

Edging

From RS with smaller hook, join A with a sl st in left side seam. **Rnd 1** Ch 1, making sure that work lies flat, sc around entire edge, working 3 sc in each corner. Join rnd with a sl st in ch-1. Fasten off.

Armhole edging

From RS with smaller hook, join A with a sl st in side seam. **Rnd 1** Ch 1, making sure that work lies flat, sc around armhole edge. Join rnd with a sl st in ch-1. Fasten off. Sew on collar.

Ties

(make 4)

With smaller hook and A, ch 36. Fasten off. Sew a pair of ties at beg of collar and the other pair 2 (2½)"/5 (6)cm below.

121

w r a p   i t   u p

SIZES

Instructions are written for size 6-12 months. Changes for size 18 months-3 years are in parentheses.

FINISHED MEASUREMENTS

Hat
• Circumference 16 (18)"/40.5 (45.5)cm
Scarf
• 4" x 32"/10 x 81cm

MATERIALS

• 1 1¾oz/50g balls (each approx 138yd/126m) of Garnstudio Karisma (wool ④) each in #41 blue (A), #20 gold (B), #26 fuchsia (C), #27 teal (D) and #12 purple (E)
• Size H/8 (5mm) crochet hook or size to obtain gauge
• Small safety pin

GAUGE

14 sts and 12 rows to 4"/10cm over hdc using size H/8 (5mm) hook.
Take time to check gauge.

NOTES

1 Hat is made on the WS, then turned RS out when crocheting is completed.
2 See page 131 for making color changes.

HAT

With A, ch 56 (64). **Foundation rnd** Taking care not to twist ch, join ch with a hdc forming a ring, then hdc in each ch to end—56 (64) sts. Mark last st made with safety pin to indicate end of rnd.
Next 1 (3) rnds Ch 2, hdc in each st around. Join rnd with a sl st in 2nd ch of ch-2, changing to B on last rnd.
Next rnd Ch 1,*sc in next st, in next st work [yo, draw up a lp, yo, draw through 2 lps on hook] 3 times, yo and draw through all 4 lps on hook (bobble made); rep from * around. Join rnd with a sl st in ch-1 changing to C.
Next 3 (5) rnds Ch 2, hdc in each st around. Join rnd with a sl st in 2nd ch of ch-2 changing to D on last rnd.

Next rnd Ch 1, *sc in next st, sk next st, work 3 dc in next st (shell made), sk next st; rep from * around. Join rnd with a sl st in ch-1 changing to E.

Next rnd Ch 3, *work 3 dc in next sc, sc in 3rd dc of next shell; rep from * around. Join rnd with a sl st in 3rd ch of ch-3 changing to A.

Next 2 (4) rnds Ch 2, hdc in each st around. Join rnd with a sl st in 2nd ch of ch-2 changing to B on last rnd.

Crown shaping

Dec rnd 1 Ch 2, *hdc in next 6 sts, dec 1 st over next 2 sts; rep from * around—49 (56) sts. Join rnd with a sl st in 2nd ch of ch-2 changing to C.

Next rnd Ch 1, sc in 1 (0) st, *bobble in next st, sc in next st; rep from * around. Join rnd with a sl st in ch-1 changing to D.

Dec rnd 2 Ch 2, *hdc in next 5 sts, dec 1 st over next 2 sts; rep from * around—42 (48) sts. Join rnd with a sl st in 2nd ch of ch-2.

Next rnd Ch 2, hdc in each st around. Join rnd with a sl st in 2nd ch of ch-2 changing to E.

Dec rnd 3 Ch 2, *hdc in next 4 sts, dec 1 st over next 2 sts; rep from * around—35 (40) sts. Join rnd with a sl st in 2nd ch of ch-2 changing to A.

Next rnd Ch 1, *sc in next st, sk next st, work 3 dc in next st (shell made), sk next st; rep from * around, end sc in 1 (0) st. Join rnd with a sl st in ch-1 changing to B.

Dec rnd 4 Ch 2, *hdc in next 3 sts, dec 1 st over next 2 sts; rep from * around—28 (32) sts. Join rnd with a sl st in 2nd ch of ch-2 changing to C.

Next rnd Ch 2, hdc in each st around. Join rnd with a sl st in 2nd ch of ch-2 changing to D.

Dec rnd 5 Ch 2, *hdc in next 2 sts, dec 1 st over next 2 sts; rep from * around—21 (24) sts. Join rnd with a sl st in 2nd ch of ch-2 changing to E.

Next rnd Ch 2, hdc in each st around. Join rnd with a sl st in 2nd ch of ch-2 changing to A.

Dec rnd 6 Ch 2, *hdc in next st, dec 1 st over next 2 sts; rep from * around—14 (16) sts. Join rnd with a sl st in 2nd ch of ch-2.

Next rnd Ch 2, hdc in each st around. Join rnd with a sl st in 2nd ch of ch-2.

Dec rnd 7 Ch 2, *dec 1 st over next 2 sts; rep from * around—7 (8) sts. Join rnd with

a sl st in 2nd ch of ch-2. Fasten off leaving a long tail. Thread tail into tapestry needle and weave through sts. Pull tight to gather; fasten off securely. Turn hat RS out.

EARFLAPS
(make 2)
With A, ch 6. **Foundation row** Hdc in 3rd ch from hook and in each ch across—4 sts. Ch 2, turn.

Inc row 1 Work 2 hdc in first st, hdc in next 2 sts, 2 hdc in last st. Join B, ch 1, turn—6 sts.

Next row Sc in first st, bobble in next st, sc in next 2 sts, bobble in next st, sc in last st. Join C, ch 2, turn.

Next row Hdc in each st across. Ch 2, turn.

Inc row 2 Work 2 hdc in first st, hdc in next 4 sts, 2 hdc in last st. Join D, ch 2, turn—8 sts.

Inc row 3 Work 2 hdc in first st, hdc in next 6 sts, 2 hdc in last st—10 sts. Ch 2, turn.

Inc row 4 Work 2 hdc in first st, hdc in next 8 sts, 2 hdc in last st. Join E, ch 1, turn—12 sts.

Next row Sc in first 2 sts, [sk next st, work 3 dc in next st, sk next st, sc in next st]

twice, sc in last 2 sts. Join A, ch 2, turn.
Next 1 (2) rows Hdc in each st across.
Ch 2, turn. After last row is completed,
fasten off.

Edging and tie
With RS facing, join D with a sc in side
edge of last row. Making sure that work
lies flat, sc along side edge to 2 center sts
of foundation row. Ch 51 (tie), then sc in
2nd ch from hook and in each ch across.
Cont to sc along side edge to last row on
opposite side. Fasten off.

FINISHING
Sew earflaps to either side of hat.
Pompom
Using all colors, make a 3"/7.5cm in
diameter pompom (see pompom
instructions). Sew pompom to top of hat.

SCARF
With A, ch 115. **Foundation row (RS)** Hdc
in 3rd ch from hook and in each ch
across—113 sts. Join B, ch 1, turn.
Row 1 Sc in first 2 sts, *work bobble in
next st, sc in next 3 sts; rep from *, end
bobble in next st, sc in last 2 sts. Join C,
ch 2, turn.

Row 2 Hdc in each st across. Join D,
ch 1, turn.
Row 3 Sc in first st, sk next st, *work 3 dc
in next st (shell), sk next st, sc in next st, sk
next st; rep from *, end work 3 dc in next
st, sk next st, sc in last st. Join E, ch 3, turn.
Row 4 Work 2 dc in first sc (half shell
made), *work 3 dc in next sc, sc in 3rd dc
of next shell; rep from *, end work 2 dc in
last sc. Join A, ch 2, turn.
Row 5 Hdc in each st across. Join B,
ch 2, turn.
Row 6 Hdc in each st across. Join C,
ch 1, turn.
Row 7 Rep row 3. Join D, ch 3, turn.
Row 8 Rep row 4. Join E, ch 1, turn.
Row 9 Rep row 1. Join A, ch 2, turn.
Row 10 Hdc in each st across. Fasten off.

FINISHING
Fringe
For each fringe, cut 4 strands of yarn
8½"/21.5cm long. Use hook to pull
through and knot fringe. Knot 11 fringe
across each end, matching fringe color to
row color.

s n u g   a s   a   b u g

FINISHED MEASUREMENTS

• 28½" x 34"/72 x 86cm (not including fringe)

MATERIALS

• 2 3½oz/100g skeins (each approx 210yd/192m) of Patons Decor (acrylic/wool ⑤) in #1633 chocolate taupe (F)
• 1 skein each in #1602 aran (A), #1658 rich rose (B), #1712 grape (C), #1641 periwinkle (D) and #1640 pale periwinkle (E)
• Size I/9 (5.5mm) crochet hook or size to obtain gauge

GAUGE

12 sts and 10 rows to 4"/10cm over hdc using size I/9 (5.5mm) hook.
Take time to check gauge.

NOTE

See page 131 for making color changes.

BLANKET

(make 2 pieces)
With A, ch 87.
Row 1 Hdc in 3rd ch from hook and in each ch across—85 sts. Join B, ch 2, turn.
Row 2 Hdc in each st across. Join C, ch 2, turn.
Row 3 Rep row 2. Join D, ch 2, turn.
Row 4 Rep row 2. Join E, ch 2, turn.
Row 5 Rep row 2. Join F, ch 2, turn.

Rows 6-9 Rep row 2. Ch 2, turn. After row 9 is completed, ch 1, turn.
Row 10 Sc in each st across. Join A, ch 3, turn.
Row 11 *Dc in next 2 sts, dc between 2 sts of row below; rep from * end, dc in last st. Join D, ch 1, turn
Row 12 Sc in first st, sk next st, *work 3 dc in next st (shell made), sk next st, sc in next st, sk next st; rep from *, end work 3 dc in next st (shell made), sk next st, sc in last st. Join E, ch 3, turn.
Row 13 Work 2 dc in first sc (half shell made), *work 3 dc in next sc, sc in 3rd dc of next shell; rep from *, end work 2 dc in last sc. Join F, ch 2, turn.
Row 14 Hdc in each sc and dc across—85 sts. Ch 2, turn.
Rows 15 and 16 Hdc in each st across. Ch 2, turn. After row 16 is completed, join A, ch 1, turn.
Row 17 Rep row 12. Join B, ch 3 turn.
Row 18 Rep row 13. Join C, ch 1, turn.
Row 19 Sc in first 2 sts, *in next st work [yo, draw up a lp, yo, draw through 2 lps on hook] 3 times, yo and draw through all 4 lps on hook (bobble made), sc in next 3 sts; rep from *, end bobble in next st, sc in last 2 sts. Join B, ch 1, turn.
Row 20 Rep row 12. Join A, ch 3, turn.
Row 21 Rep row 13. Join F, ch 2, turn.
Row 22 Rep row 14.
Rows 23-25 Hdc in each st across. Ch 2,

turn. After row 25 is completed, join A, ch 1, turn.

Rows 26-29 Rep rows 11-14. Ch 2, turn.

Rows 30-33 Hdc in each st across. Ch 2, turn. After row 33 is completed, join A, ch 1, turn.

Rows 34 and 35 Sc in each st across. Ch 1, turn. After row 35 is completed, join B, ch 2, turn.

Rows 36 and 37 Hdc in each st across. Ch 2, turn. After row 37 is completed, join C, ch 2, turn.

Rows 38 Hdc in each st across. Join D, ch 2, turn.

Rows 39 and 40 Hdc in each st across. Ch 2, turn. After row 41 is completed, join E, ch 2, turn.

Row 41 Hdc in each st across. Join F, ch 2, turn.

Row 42 Hdc in each st across. Fasten off.

FINISHING

Sew pieces tog.

Fringe

For each fringe, cut 3 strands of B 8"/20cm long. Use hook to pull through and knot fringe. Knot 42 fringe across each end.

SIZES

Instructions are written for size 3-6 months. Changes for sizes 9-12 months, 18-24 months and 3 years are in parentheses.

FINISHED MEASUREMENTS

• Chest 18 (20, 22, 24)"/45.5 (51, 56, 61)cm

MATERIALS

• 2 (3, 3, 4) 1¾oz/50g balls (each approx 136yd/124m) of Patons Grace (cotton ③) in #60409 ruby
• Size F/5 (3.75mm) crochet hook or size to obtain gauge
• ½ (⅔, 1, 1) yd/.5 (.75, 1, 1)m of 45"/114cm wide lavender Dupioni silk
• 1yd/1m of beaded fringe (optional)
• Matching sewing threads

GAUGE

5 shells and 10 rows to 4"/10cm over pat st using size F/5 (3.75mm) hook.
Take time to check gauge.

SHELL STITCH PATTERN

(multiple of 4 sts plus 1)

Row 1 Sc in first st, sk next st, *work 3 dc in next st (shell made), sk next st, sc in next st, sk next st; rep from *, end work 3 dc in next st (shell made), sk next st, sc in last st. Ch 3, turn.
Row 2 Work 2 dc in first sc (half shell made), *work 3 dc in next sc, sc in 3rd dc of next shell; rep from *, end work 2 dc in last sc. Ch 1, turn.
Row 3 Sc in first dc of half shell, *work 3 dc in next sc, sc in 3rd dc of next shell; rep from *, end work 3 dc in last sc, sc in 2nd dc of half shell. Ch 3, turn.
Rep rows 2 and 3 for pat st.

BACK BODICE

Ch 46 (50, 58, 62). **Foundation row** Sc in 2nd ch from hook and in each ch across—45 (49, 57, 61) sts. Ch 1, turn. Work row 1 of pat st—11 (12, 14, 15) whole shells. Work row 2 of pat st—10 (11, 13, 14) whole shells and 2 half-shells. Cont in pat st and work even for 1 (3, 4, 6) rows, end ready for row 2 (2, 3, 3). Fasten off. Turn work.

Armhole shaping

Next row Sk first whole shell, join yarn with a sl st in next sc, ch 3, work 2 dc in same st (half shell), work to within sc of last whole shell, work 2 dc in this sc. Ch 1, turn—8 (9, 10, 11) whole shells and 2 half-shells. Beg with row 3 for all sizes, work even for 2 (4, 4, 4) rows, end ready for row 3.

Left neck shaping

Next row Sc in first dc of half shell, [work 3 dc in next sc, sc in 3rd dc of next shell] 2 (2, 3, 3) times. Ch 3, turn. Work even until armhole measures 3 (3½, 4, 4½)"/7.5 (9, 10, 11.5)cm. Fasten off.

Right neck shaping

Next row Sk 4 (5, 4, 5) center shells, join yarn with a sc in 3rd dc of next shell, work to end. Cont to work as for left neck.

FRONT BODICE

Work as for back bodice.

FINISHING

Sew shoulder and side seams. Cut beaded fringe to fit around lower edge of bodice, then add 1"/2.5cm for overlap. Hand-sew to WS of lower edge of bodice.

Skirt

From fabric, cut 2 skirt pieces each 15 (16, 18, 19)"/38 (40.5, 45.5, 48)cm x 20 (22, 23, 26)"/51 (56, 58.5, 66)cm. With RS tog and using ½"/13mm seam allowance sew

side seams. Gather one long edge of skirt, adjust gathers to fit; hand-sew to lower edge of bodice. Press ¼"/6mm to WS along rem long edge of skirt, then hem to desired length.

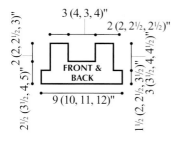

3 (4, 3, 4)"
2 (2, 2½, 2½)"
2 (2, 2½, 3)"
2½ (3½, 4, 5)"
FRONT & BACK
1½ (2, 2½, 3½)"
3 (3½, 4, 4½)"
9 (10, 11, 12)"

THE SLIP KNOT

1 Begin to crochet by making a slip knot. Make a loop several inches [or centimeters] from the end of the yarn. Insert the hook through the loop and catch the tail with the end.

2 Pull the yarn through the loop on the hook.

CROCHET HOOKS

AUS	METRIC
14 steel	.60mm
12 steel	.75mm
10 steel	1.00mm
6 steel	1.50mm
5 steel	1.75mm
B/1	2.00mm
C/2	2.50mm
D/3	3.00mm
E/4	3.50mm
F/5	4.00mm
G/6	4.50mm
H/8	5.00mm
I/9	5.50mm
J/10	6.00mm
	6.50mm
K/10.5	7.00mm

SIZING

Most of the garments in this book are written for sizes from six months to three years old, allowing extra ease for your child to grow into the garment. Since children's measurements change so rapidly, it is best to measure your child or a sweater that fits well to determine which size to make.

YARN SELECTION

For an exact reproduction of the projects photographed, use the yarn listed in the "Materials" section of the pattern. We've chosen yarns that are readily available in the U.S. and Canada at the time of printing. The Resources list on page136 provides addresses of yarn distributors. Contact them for the name of a retailer in your area.

YARN SUBSTITUTION

You may wish to substitute yarns. Perhaps you view small-scale projects as a chance to incorporate leftovers from your yarn stash, or the yarn specified may not be available in your area. You'll need to crochet to the given gauge to obtain the crocheted measurements with a substitute yarn (see "Gauge" on this page). Be sure to consider how the fiber content of the substitute yarn will affect the comfort and the ease of care of your projects.

To facilitate yarn substitution, yarns are graded by the standard stitch gauge obtained in single crochet. You'll find a grading number in the "Materials" section of the pattern, immediately following the fiber type of the yarn. Look for a substitute yarn that falls into the same category. The suggested hook size and gauge on the yarn label should be comparable to that on the "Yarn Symbols" chart (see page 131).

After you've successfully gauge-swatched a substitute yarn, you'll need to figure out how much of the substitute yarn the project requires. First, find the total length of the original yarn in the pattern (multiply number of balls by yards/meters per ball). Divide this figure by the new yards/meters per ball (listed on the yarn label). Round up to the next whole number. The answer is the number of balls required.

GAUGE

It is always important to crochet a gauge swatch, and it is even more so with garments to ensure proper fit.

Patterns usually state gauge over a 4"/10cm span, however it's beneficial to make a larger test swatch. This gives a more precise stitch gauge, a better idea of the appearance and drape of the crocheted fabric, and gives you a chance to familiarize yourself with the stitch pattern.

The type of hook used—wood or metal—will influence gauge, so crochet your swatch with the hook you plan to use for the project. Try different hook sizes until your sample measures the required number of stitches and rows. To get fewer stitches to the inch/cm, use a larger hook; to get more stitches to the inch/cm, use a smaller hook.

It's a good idea to keep your gauge swatch in order to test blocking and cleaning methods.

FOLLOWING CHARTS

Charts are a convenient way to follow colorwork patterns at a glance. When crocheting back and forth in rows, read charts from right to left on right side (RS) rows and from left to right on wrong side (WS) rows, repeating any stitch and row repeats as directed in the pattern. Posting a self-adhesive note under your working row is an easy way to keep track of your place.

COLORWORK CROCHETING

Three main types of colorwork are explored in this book: stripes, intarsia and stranding.

Stripes

When working in single crochet, change color at the end of the row by drawing the new color through 2 loops on hook to complete the last single crochet, then chain and turn.

For half double crochet, draw new color through 3 loops on hook to complete last half double crochet, then chain and turn.

When working in double crochet, draw new color through last 2 loops on hook to complete last double crochet, then chain and turn.

To prevent lumpy seams, do not make knots when changing colors. Instead, leave a long tail of yarn, then weave in tails after piece is completed and before sewing garment together.

Intarsia

All the Argyle designs are worked with separate bobbins of individual colors so there are no long strands of yarn. When changing color, pick up new color from under dropped color to prevent holes.

Stranding

When changing colors at the beginning of rows or rounds, carry yarn along for a few rows only, or cut yarn and rejoin when needed. It is important to keep the floats small and neat so they don't catch on small fingers when the garment is pulled on.

BLOCKING

Blocking is a crucial finishing step in the crocheting process. It is the best way to shape pattern pieces and smooth crocheted edges in preparation for sewing together. Most garments retain their shape if the blocking stages in the instructions are followed carefully. Choose a blocking method according to the instructions on the yarn care label, and when in doubt, test-block your gauge swatch.

Wet Block Method

Using rust-proof pins, pin pieces to measurements on a flat surface and lightly dampen using a spray bottle. Allow to dry before removing pins.

Steam Block Method

With wrong sides facing, pin pieces. Steam lightly, holding the iron 2"/5cm above the crocheting. Do not press or it will flatten stitches.

CARE

Refer to the yarn label for the recommended cleaning method. Many of the projects in the book can be either washed by hand, or in the machine on a gentle or wool cycle, using lukewarm water

CHAIN

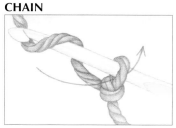

1 Pass yarn over the hook and catch it with the hook.

2 Draw yarn through the loop on the hook.

3 Repeat steps 1 and 2 to make a chain.

YARN SYMBOLS

③ Medium Weight
(18-22 stitches per 4"/10cm)
Includes DK and worsted, the most commonly used knitting yarns.
The range of hook sizes is F-G

④ Medium-heavy Weight
(16-18 stitches per 4"/10cm)
Also called heavy worsted or Aran.
The range of hook sizes is G-H

⑤ Bulky Weight
(13-16 stitches per 4"/10cm)
Also called chunky. Includes heavier Icelandic yarns.
The range of hook sizes is H-I

⑥ Extra-bulky Weight
(9-12 stitches per 4"/10cm)
The heaviest yarns available.
The range of hook sizes is J and up

SINGLE CROCHET

1 Insert hook through top two loops of a stitch. Pass yarn over hook and draw up a loop—two loops on hook.

2 Pass yarn over hook and draw through both loops on hook.

3 Continue in the same way, inserting hook into each stitch.

with a mild detergent. Do not agitate or soak for more than 10 minutes. Rinse gently with tepid water, then fold in a towel and gently press the water out. Lay flat to dry, away from excess heat and light. Check the yarn label for any specific care instructions such as dry cleaning or tumble drying.

CROCHETING GLOSSARY

decrease 1 dc [Yo. Insert hook into next st and draw up a lp. Yo and draw through 2 lps] twice, yo and draw through all 3 lps on hook.

decrease 1 hdc [Yo, insert hook into next st and draw up a lp] twice, yo and draw through all 5 lps on hook.

decrease 1 sc [Insert hook into next st and draw up a lp] twice, yo and draw through all 3 lps on hook.

increase 1 stitch Work 2 sts in 1 st.

join yarn with a dc Make a slip knot, then yo. Insert hook into st. Yo and draw up a lp. [Yo and draw through 2 lps on hook] twice.

join yarn with a hdc Make a slip knot, then yo. Insert hook into st. Yo and draw up a lp. Yo and draw through 3 lps on hook.

join yarn with a sc Make a slip knot. Insert hook into st. Yo and draw up a lp. Yo and draw through 2 lps on hook.

join yarn with a sl st Make a slip knot. Insert hook into st. Yo and draw up a lp and draw through lp on hook.

GRANNY SQUARE BASICS

GRANNY SQUARE

(multi-color)

Ch 4. Join ch with a sl st forming a ring.

Rnd 1 (RS) Ch 3 (always counts as 1 dc), work 2 dc over ring, ch 2, * work 3 dc over ring, ch 2; rep from * 3 times. Join rnd with a sl st in 3rd ch of ch-3. Fasten off. From WS, join next color with a sl st in any ch-2 sp.

Rnd 2 Ch 3, work 2 dc in same ch-2 sp, ch 1, * work (3 dc, ch 2, 3 dc) in next ch-2 sp, ch 1; rep from * 3 times, end with 3 dc in beg ch-2 sp, ch 2. Join rnd with a sl st in 3rd ch of ch-3. Fasten off. From RS, join next color with a sl st in any ch-2 sp.

Rnd 3 Ch 3, work 2 dc in same ch-2 sp, ch 1, * work 3 dc in next ch-1 sp, ch 1, work (3 dc, ch 2, 3 dc) in next ch-2 sp, ch 1; rep from * 3 times, end with 3 dc in next ch-1 sp, ch 1, 3

CROCHET ABBREVIATIONS		
approx approximately	**lp(s)** loop(s)	**tog** together
beg begin(ning)	**m** meter(s)	**tr** treble crochet (UK: dtr double treble)
CC contrasting color	**mm** millimeter(s)	
ch chain(s)	**MC** main color	**WS** wrong side(s)
cont continu(e)(ing)	**oz** ounce(s)	**yd** yard(s)
dc double crochet (UK: tr treble)	**pat(s)** pattern(s)	**yo** yarn over
	rem remain(s)(ing)	* = repeat directions following * as many times as indicated.
dec decrease(ing) (see glossary)	**rep** repeat	
	rnd(s) round(s)	[ ] = repeat directions inside brackets as many times as indicated.
g gram(s)	**RS** right side(s)	
hdc half double crochet (UK: htr half treble)	**sc** single crochet (UK: dc double crochet)	( ) = work directions contained inside parentheses in st indicated.
	sk skip	
inc increase(e)(ing) (see glossary)	**sl** slip	
	sl st slip st (UK: sc single crochet)	
	st(s) stitch(es)	

dc in beg ch-2 sp, ch 2. Join rnd with a sl st in 3rd ch of ch-3. Fasten off. From WS, join next color with a sl st in any ch-2 sp.

Rnd 4 Ch 3, work 2 dc in same ch-2 sp, ch 1, * [work 3 dc in next ch-1 sp, ch 1] twice, work (3 dc, ch 2, 3 dc) in next ch-2 sp, ch 1; rep from * 3 times, end with [work 3 dc in next ch-1 sp, ch 1] twice, 3 dc in beg ch-2 sp, ch 2. Join rnd with a sl st in 3rd ch of ch-3. Fasten off. From RS, join next color with a sl st in any ch-2 sp.

Rnd 5 Ch 3, work 2 dc in same ch-2 sp, ch 1, * [work 3 dc in next ch-1 sp, ch 1] 3 times, work (3 dc, ch 2, 3 dc) in next ch-2 sp, ch 1; rep from * 3 times, end with [work 3 dc in next ch-1 sp, ch 1] 3 times, 3 dc in beg ch-2 sp, ch 2. Join rnd with a sl st in 3rd ch of ch-3. Fasten off leaving a long tail for sewing.

GRANNY SQUARE
(solid color)

Ch 4. Join ch with a sl st forming a ring.

Rnd 1 (RS) Ch 3 (always counts as 1 dc), work 2 dc over ring, ch 1, * work 3 dc over ring, ch 1; rep from * 3 times. Join rnd with a sl st in 3rd ch of ch-3. Turn.

Rnd 2 Ch 3, work (2 dc, ch 2, 3dc) in first ch-1 sp, ch 1, * work (3 dc, ch 1, 3 dc) in next ch-1 sp, ch 1; rep from * 3 times. Join rnd with a sl st in 3rd ch of ch-3. Fasten off leaving a long tail for sewing.

HALF-GRANNY
(multi-color)

Ch 3. Join ch with a sl st formng a ring.

Row 1 (RS) Ch 4 (counts as 1 dc and ch-1), work (3 dc, ch 2, 3 dc) over ring, ch 1, dc over ring, joining next color. Ch 3, turn.

Row 2 Work 3 dc in first ch-1 sp, ch 1, work (3 dc, ch 2, 3 dc) in ch-2 sp, ch 1, work 3 dc in last ch-1 sp. Fasten off leaving a long tail for sewing.

HALF-GRANNY
(solid color)

Ch 3. Join ch with a sl st formng a ring.

Row 1 (RS) Ch 4 (counts as 1 dc and ch-1), work (3 dc, ch 2, 3 dc) over ring, ch 1, dc over ring. Ch 3, turn.

Row 2 Work 3 dc in first ch-1 sp, ch 1, work (3 dc, ch 2, 3 dc) in ch-2 sp, ch 1, work 3 dc in last ch-1 sp. Fasten off leaving a long tail for sewing.

QUARTER-GRANNY
(solid color)

Ch 3. Join ch with a sl st formng a ring.

Row 1 (RS) Ch 3 (counts as 1 dc), work (2 dc, ch 2, 3 dc) over ring. Fasten off leaving a long tail for sewing.

HALF-DOUBLE CROCHET

1 Pass yarn over hook. Insert hook through the top two loops of a stitch.

2 Pass yarn over hook and draw up a loop—three loops on hook. Pass yarn over hook.

3 Draw through all three loops on hook.

DOUBLE CROCHET

1 Pass yarn over hook. Insert hook through the top two loops of a stitch.

2 Pass yarn over hook and draw up a loop—three loops on hook.

3 Pass yarn over hook and draw it through the first two loops on the hook, pass yarn over hook and draw through the remaining two loops. Continue in the same way, inserting hook into each stitch.

CHAIN STITCH

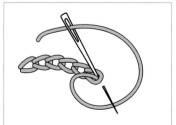

a c k n o w l e d g e m e n t s

I started working on this book before I realized it was even a book. I sketched little garments, stacked up balls of yarn to see various color combinations, but most of all, I watched the adorable kids in my neighborhood. So first off, I'd like to thank Jacob, Samantha, Jack, Katie, Michael, Lindsey, Scottie, Claire, Amitie and little Katie for their incredible inspiration, and I'd like to thank their wonderful parents who offered their support.

Many thanks to the crocheters—Mary Fletcher, Kathleen Stuart, Klaudia Povincova, Greta Huhutala, and Faith Ragan—who translated my thoughts into reality. A special thanks to Veronica "Pinka" Peck, who not only crocheted but also sent my original message out to the BARC

Guild and as many people possible. I don't know the names of these people who helped spread the word, but thanks to all of you as well.

None of this would have been possible without the support, love and encouragement of my husband, Tom Noggle. He is always in my corner and keeps me laughing through hard times. Hugs to my daughter Heather who managed to become a creative, kind, intelligent and loving person while raising me. My son Jonathan, who loved whatever I made for him and wore them until they were tattered and way too small. My Mom, Jean Jensen, for passing on her creative genes and staying up all those nights sewing for me. There has also been one person who always understood my creativity and the chaos that spins around me, and managed to love me anyway-my sister Rajeana. Thank you for believing in me. I also want to give a heartfelt thanks to my good friend Dorothy, who has taught me what true friendship is all about.

Finally, I'd like to thank the people and staff at Sixth&Spring Books who are responsible for making me look good. Theresa McKeon, who understood my vision and set the course for this book, all the while being kind and supportive. Veronica Manno for her help with the finishing details and Carla Scott for making sense of it all. Pat Harste for her amazing editorial eye and ability to make my patterns work. Chi Ling Moy who is an absolute genius at book design and art direction. Dan Howell for his expert photographic eye and Mary Hampton Helt for her wonderful fashion styling sense. And a very special thanks to Trisha Malcolm who understood what I was talking about when I approached her with the idea for this book. Without her, none of this would have been possible.

r e s o u r c e s

Aurora Yarns
P.O. Box 3068
Moss Beach, Ca 94038

Berroco, Inc.
P.O. Box 367
Uxbridge, MA 01569

Brown Sheep Co., Inc.
100662 Country Toad 16
Mitchell, NE 69357

Classic Elite Yarns
300 A Jackson Street
Bldg. #5
Lowell, MA 01852

Coats & Clark
Attn: Consumer Service
P.O. Box 12229
Greenville, SC 29612-0229
www.coatsandclark.com

Friends, Inc.
P.O. Box 2134
Everett, WA 98203

Garnstudio
Distributed by Aurora Yarns

K1C2, LLC
2220 Eastman Ave. #105
Ventura, CA 93003

Knitting Fever, Inc.
P.O. Box 502
Roosevelt, NY 11575

Noro
Distributed by Knitting Fever, Inc.

Patons
P.O. Box 40
Listowel, ON N4W3H3
www.patonsyarns.com

Red Heart
Distributed by Coats & Clark

Tahki•Stacy Charles, Inc.
8000 Cooper Ave., Bldg 1
Glendale, NY 11385
Email: info@tahkistacycharles.com

Wendy
Distributed by Berroco, Inc.